HOUSEHOLD STORIES
Katei Monogatari

a love story with a difference

Angela Jeffs

Cover: (Japan has three alphabets, traditionally written vertically and from right to left. Today there is more laxity.) The four large ideographic characters scribed vertically on the right, known as *kanji*, read as KA-TEI-MONO-GATARI. Under the main title, the title is also given in in *romaji* (the phonetic spelling of Japanese in the English alpahabet), and then, below, *hiragana* (phonetic *nihongo*, the Japanese language). The author's name is given in English and *katakana*, the alphabet used to spell out all foreign words, so reading phonetically as a-n-je-ra-je-fu-su.

Published by Angela Jeffs

Copyright © Angela Jeffs

First edition 2017

Second edition 2018

ISBN: 13:978-1974389919 (CreateSpace assigned)
ISBN: 10:197438991X

BISAC – General/Memoir

Printed to order by CreateSpace on Amazon.com

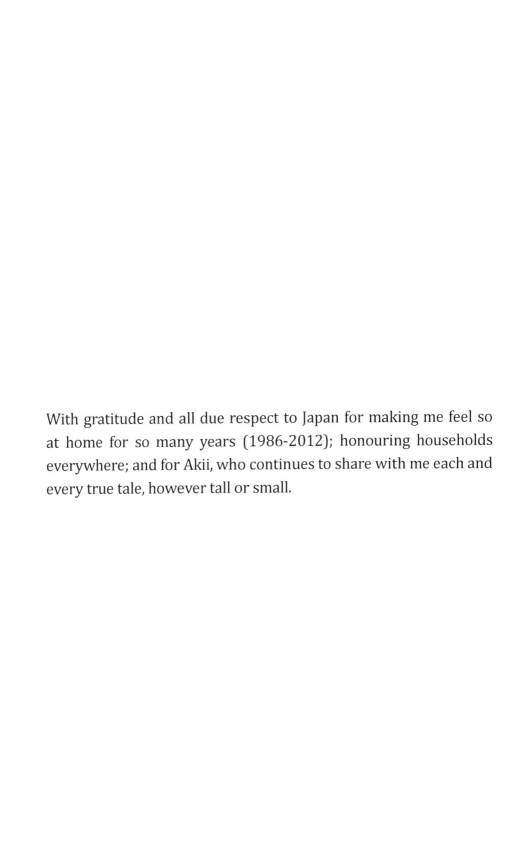

With gratitude and all due respect to Japan for making me feel so at home for so many years (1986-2012); honouring households everywhere; and for Akii, who continues to share with me each and every true tale, however tall or small.

RETROSPECTIVELY . . .

I have always been a more enthusiastic party-giver than party-goer. But there are exceptions. Which was why, in the late spring of 2004, I was to be found hanging out at a launch party held opposite the Korean Embassy in Moto-Azabu, Tokyo. I was living in Japan at the time.

It celebrated the opening of a new kind of arts centre by three remarkable women, one Californian (Kristin), one Japanese (Mayumi), and the third American-Thai-Filipina (Lia). It was a venue where anyone could learn to draw, sculpt, play the piano and journal visually via right-brain (as opposed to left-brain) techniques. Hence its curious name: RBR, for Right Brain Research.

On invitation, I began drop-in classes in creative writing based on home-grown experimental exercises that would trick the left-brain — that masculine-inclined lobe that tells us we cannot write and never will be able to write, so why bother to even try — into shutting up/down, so allowing the intuitive and creative feminine right-brain to function freely.

We all used to be so much more right-brain before the macho Ancient Greeks got their reasoned hands on us and laid down the linear system of Western-style education that is still adhered to today. Sadly, the days when we communed naturally with the gods have given way to the three Rs (reading, 'riting and 'rithmatic) and all the laws of logic and rationale.

By 2005, the classes, initially offered through trial and error, had evolved into an eight-week course: Drawing On The Writer Within. At the end of this, students asked when the next one would begin. Today, DOTWW offers a four-level programme: Initiation, Exploration, Affirmation and Confirmation.

The first three levels consist of weekly exercises followed by a 25-minute session of Proprioceptive Writing and *omiyage*, a Japanese word meaning a semi-obligatory gift or souvenir. In this instance, I offer students the gift of a writing task to do in their own time ahead of the next session, to be shared — gifted back — for constructive feedback.

Level 4 is different. For omiyage, students are asked to plan, develop and begin work on an eight-week project rather than weekly assignments. This is to encourage their internal resources of self-discipline as writers. After all, at the end of this course, they are — theoretically, at least — on their own.

To encourage them and (having spent years in journalism, which requires a more restrictive skill set) to plumb my own creative depths, I began a project of my own. The book that follows evolved from this self-imposed exercise.

I began Household Stories (*Katei Monogatari*) in the autumn of

2010, by which time RBR had moved on and into new premises. I was working with six women — American, Scottish and English DOTWW graduates — all of whom had completed the first three levels. I completed my own first draft a year later, by which time circumstances had changed.

While now a testament to what has gone before, it remains as intensely personal as the time in which it was tip-tapped into life. Welcome, therefore, to a story written in the present in the past.

SCOTLAND, 2016

Note:

All names are written in the Western manner. (Traditionally, Japanese family names are given first, followed by the given name, e.g., Ueda Yasuyuki).

Since the book can be read in two ways, either from beginning to end as you move through the house, or by dipping in, room by room, words in Japanese are printed the first time in each section in italics, and thereafter as part of the text.

Some Japanese words are now part and parcel of everyday language in the English-speaking world and can be found in most English-language dictionaries: tsunami, kimono, sushi, geisha, sake, futon, samurai, for example. I have left these as running text.

Where there are long vowels, they are duplicated, except with unfamiliar phonetics like rohka (for corridor), where an 'h' indicates the 'o' sound is extended. The use of 'u' is more contemporary, but 'h' makes the book consistent with the spelling of authors' names under Recommended Reading on page 240. In more familiar words like Tokyo and Kyoto (actually Tohkyoh and Kyohto) the long vowel is not noted.

There is a glossary at the back to refer to if and when required.

If you can think of life, for a moment,
as a large house with a nursery,
living and dining rooms, bedrooms, study, and so forth,
all unfamiliar and bright,
the chapters which follow are, in a way,
like looking through the windows of this house.
Certain occupants will be glimpsed only briefly.
Visitors come and go.
At some windows you may wish to stay longer, but alas,
As with any house, all within cannot be seen.
James Salter

CONTENTS

ANOTHER TIME, ANOTHER PLACE

Is a house a hook? Meaning, is it offering enough encouragement for the active book browser to be drawn in and advance to the next step: beg, borrow or buy — preferably buy — a copy.

Maybe it will help make up your mind that the house is in Japan. A Japanese hook.

Here's hoping . . .

* * *

"Now for this week's *omiyage . . .* " I proffered the first Level 3 group of DOTWW writing students way back in 2007: "Write a love story."

As previously explained, omiyage is a more-or-less obligatory gift. In this case, I offer an assignment as a gift; students then gift back what they write.

In this particular instance the accounts, yearnings, yarns and fairy tales they created over the next seven days in their own time and places of imaginative wordsmithing. A wondrous mix of darkness, tenderness, humour, regret and celebration. Plus a few vividly erotic dollops of sex.

Following on, I charged the first Level 4 course members with a project of their own rather than designated weekly assignments. I had helped raise them as fledgling writers over twenty-four weeks and innumerable meets and retreats, and now it was time to prove they could fly. Their wings were strong; they just needed that final fillip of confidence to lift off and keep going. As a famed Zen adage encourages with one hundred percent faith: *Leap and the net will catch you.*

Wanting to write something of my own to act as a supportive

pacemaker, I considered which of the themes set over the years beckoned at that particular point in my life.

Which is why, no sooner had I got home than I began tapping out a love story of my own. Little to no sex, I'm afraid, but concerning my love for the house called home for the previous eight years, the life in that house, and the people who, in passing through and contributing, made such a richly rewarding life possible.

I had after all spent the previous decade writing a travelogue – an epic memoir that linked three continents and three countries sharing borders. I was ready for something nearer to hand and — if such a thing were possible — even closer to my heart.

So this is what I offer one year on: a simple love story, no more, no less. Because we may not be here much longer, and even if we stay in Japan, life is shifting, the world is in transition, and I want to remember . . .

Remember it all.

ZUSHI, 2011

*Collect things you love,
that are authentic to you,
and your house becomes
your story.*
Erin Flett

ON THE MAP
chizu de

The house, and the rooms of the house that I am about to describe, are a mix of traditional Japanese architecture and interior design (*washitsu*) and what is described in this country as Western style (*yohshitsu*).

By 'this country' I mean Japan. The house is in Honshu, Japan's largest island, and more specifically in Zushi, a small resort town on the Pacific coast, across Sagami Bay from Mt Fuji, where we have lived since 2002. South of Tokyo and Yokohama, it can be found next to Kamakura, which as a major tourist destination is always on the map.

By a mix of East and West, I mean that the house — constructed in 1960, which makes it old by contemporary Japanese standards — blends tradition with convenience. Designed to minimize the

1

barrier between inside and outside, most homes built before post-war reconstruction were dark and elemental, which while cool in summer were more often than not very cold in winter.

It is a big house. Everyone tells us so. Especially for two people, they say, with equal measures of criticism, envy and deliberate detachment in their voices.

We refuse to feel guilty. If people elect to live in the city — cramped and expensive accommodations being the rule rather than the exception — then that is their choice. We choose the one-hour commute from central Tokyo (Yokohama being halfway between); they choose convenience — a word that (like *kawaii*, for 'cute') is fast taking over all common sense and sensibility, and not only in Japan.

Yes, there are times when working or socialising that I wish I didn't have to leave early to catch the train home, but — apart from the sense of relief to be leaving the country's No. 1 hotspot for a well-overdue major earthquake — there is that moment of bliss when I walk down into the night at Zushi Station. I can smell the sea, and the sky is full of stars.

Then I remember once again why I choose to live here, and not there. Nor indeed anywhere else . . . for the time being at least.

So back to the house, designed and constructed to accommodate the needs of the kind of extended family which fifty years ago was culturally commonplace. When we first moved in and found ourselves bemused by the arrangement of electrical points, the plethora of tangled cables in virtually every room, our honourable landlady Asano-san (Mrs Asano, which sounds odd to me after so many years) was happy to explain.

"We all lived together," she said, meaning she and her husband and their children, plus her parents and his own. Parents and in-laws needed rooms of their own, with their own electrical devices while sharing basic facilities; the family spread through the rest.

They must have been reasonably affluent. Even assuming the land was owned, the house must have cost a fair amount to design and build. It is solid, with no apparent expense spared on the use of wood throughout, not only for the main structure, but also in the floors and panelling.

The roof space is enormous, and Akii — who in 2008 climbed around inside to investigate the family of racoons that had nested above my study — reported a marvellous arrangement of traditionally jointed posts and beams, with nary a nail or screw in sight. The roof tiles, *kawara*, are grey and curved and fit together like peas in a pod. It is all very fine, well chosen and well made.

Asano-san spared nothing in making us welcome. The hardwood floors shone with polish; the *tatami* mats were new and sweet-smelling, the *fusuma* (sliding doors between rooms and facing cupboards) renewed, and the *shohji* papered screens still damp with glue. It was as spick and span as she could make it, for an old house.

She was sad to leave. It had been her home; she had brought up her family there. But, one by one, her parents and in-laws died. Her children married and left home. Then her husband passed away. When her son invited her to go and live with his family down in the town below, it was not hard to decide: she was lonely. But still there was a reluctance.

We told her to visit any time. To simply just come and sit in the garden if she ever felt the need or want.

When she does call (by appointment and with gifts, for it is not the Japanese way to simply turn up unannounced and empty-handed), she is always bowled over, exclaiming over and over again how lovely everything looks, and how happy she is that we are happy.

It helps that I like flowers, trees and shrubs; the garden was her pride and joy. We have on occasion walked around together, commenting on this and that — how beautiful her white magnolia is looking this year, how well my English-style herb garden is coming along.

Every tenant should be so lucky.

To have such a landlady.

To have such a house.

THE APPROACH
shinnyuuro

… is up a slope, off a road without name. Up a cleft between two hills called just that: Yamanone, root of the mountain, mountain's root. The fact that it is an unnamed slope wider than the aforementioned unnamed road makes no sense to the uninitiated. Without street names, and with the numbering erratic, how do people find their way around? But this is Japan, and the perception of cultural mores by those who are unfamiliar with them is irrelevant, does not apply.

So, a sloping driveway off a road that is not only without a name, but also barred to vehicles other than bikes — and the cars owned by the people who laid down that particular rule in the first place. Hence the reason the house came so cheap.

The story in brief: in 2002, a kind and immensely patient Japanese man was searching for a new home for his difficult foreign wife. She, being English and a writer, wanted a room of her own to work in, and a garden.

Oh, and she had to be surrounded by green, because that was why they were giving up on the home they had lived in in Hayama for twelve years, a few miles along the coast: what she regarded as the wanton destruction of all that was beautiful — demolishing the two-hundred-year-old house opposite their rather less impressive but still lovely dwelling, clear-cutting an ancient garden — in the name of commercial profit.

Yes, she understood that families needed homes. But did all the old and lovely trees have to be sacrificed in the process? And did the twenty new houses crammed onto the site have to be quite so goddamn ugly?

So, there he was, a Japanese man in his early fifties who inevitably when introducing himself to non-Japanese, would say, "Call me Akii." Cycling around realtors, he was down to his last hope. "Do you have a house to rent?" he enquired, really feeling quite desperate and at his wits' end.

Initially the reply was in the negative, but then the agent looked from the enquirer — casually scruffy clothing, longish hair and beard — to the rusty (but trusty) bike parked outside the window, and asked in a tone that implied maybe he already knew the answer, "Do you have a car?"

My husband shook his head.

"In that case," the realtor said triumphantly, reaching down to a file under his desk, "We have a house!"

And this is it: Yamanone 3-3-3. Possibly meaning the third house on the third street on the third block, but not necessarily, as numbering can relate to the order in which houses are built. Whichever, logic comes to a standstill, because, as has already been intimated, finding your way around is not that easy; passengers in taxis invariably have to tell drivers the way. There is a second third block in Yamanone, but that is over the hill.

Are you beginning to get the picture? This is a country that by accident or design is still in many ways determined to remain inaccessible, on just about every level: culturally, linguistically, and geographically. Well, it makes sense if you want to maintain your privacy and keep intruders at bay. Japan did that with a fair degree of success (seclusionist policies of 1639–1854 leading the way) and old habits die hard.

The family at the top of our sloping approach without a name fought for some forty years to keep even close neighbours from invading their territory. Facing uphill, the steep hillside on the right — covered with flowering camellias run rampant, bamboo, cedar trees and tangles of wild wisteria together with half the land designated as roadway — was their own by inheritance; the rest belonged to the city. The rubber wheels of cars and bikes could therefore use the city's half of the road, but not the difficult neighbours' half.

Madness indeed, but they had the law on their side and that was that. Over the years, as people became more and more mobile, with expectations of convenience riding in tandem, residents of the mountain slope began to move away, leaving empty homes — old wooden buildings and even stronger structures that Nature quickly took back with vegetation and wildlife. (Hence the racoons, initially imported from America for sale as pets, but now gone native!)

My husband signed on the dotted line — accepting the clause that forbade us to have a car, even though we would have a drive large enough to accommodate half a dozen. The slope was quiet — well, of course it was — and there was green enough for a jungle. Perfect.

So he was happy, mostly (it must be said) because his wife was happy. But really, neither could believe their luck. Especially when the owner agreed to drop the rent to meet what they had been paying previously. The house had been empty for six months and she was desperate: no Japanese would rent it because all Japanese had cars. Not wholly accurate, but through experience believed to be true.

To give Difficult Family their due, they did give us special dispensation to use a car when we moved in. It would have been a bit of problem if they had not! What would we have done? Dropped in our belongings — seventy boxes full — by helicopter?

The power behind Difficult Family watched our movements from his window at the top of the slope, as he was to do daily until his recent death— we are presuming here, because one day he was not there, and DF stopped being quite so quarrelsome.

In fact, just yesterday a friend drove her enormous car right up to our door to collect her baby, and there was no reaction at all.

In the old days, there would have been a call from Asano-san: DF had phoned the real estate staff about a rare taxi or unexpected and un-forewarned-of visitor — even once, an ambulance! — after which they had called our endlessly patient landlady to pass on the complaint. It was all very trying.

But on the odd occasion when aggressive elements would shake their fist at an old man's intolerance, his last battle against progress, I would beg for clemency. It was a sad thing, I still believe. Sad that anyone should truly believe they own anything in this world; sad that he found the need to define his small, and no doubt shrinking, world with such power plays.

I wonder how he became so disturbed, so unwilling to compromise, so fearful of losing the little he believed he had. Are we all this way? To some degree, for sure.

Moving up the slope towards our address, we pass a long wall, another wall, and then a shortish flight of stone steps leading up to the Itos' house, and Samurai-san's pad to their right.

The Ito family — Yuta, Sonia and Julia, of whom much more later — are our dearest friends. Being younger — in Julia's case, much younger! — they are active, busy with careers and family life, international in outlook.

By contrast, Samurai-san has not been seen in Western clothing for years; these days he is *nihonjin* (a Japanese person) through and through. Teaching *kenjutsu* swordsmanship as an ancient military art, he travels much of the time, so is rarely here. But when spotted, we all marvel that someone so tall and handsome and classically elegant could step out of such a dump; the old wooden house really is falling about his ears, with rusted bicycles out front, and even a vintage motorbike with collapsed tyres, all gathering cobwebs.

He came once to an event in The House (our house) and as he strode through those gathered, they parted silently. It is not often one has a samurai visiting, not these days anyway.

We do wonder where he goes when not in Zushi. Nara, it has been whispered, but really he is quite the mystery man.

Does Nonaka-san know him any better? It is her entranceway we pass next, just before our own. She has never come into our house, only as far as the entrance; we are never invited into hers.

When we first arrived, her mother was still alive, but bedridden until her death, so we never saw her.

Nonaka-san herself is never well; she carries a portable oxygen tank outside, even when she goes shopping. Some days are better than others, we quickly gauge. One day she might smile and say good morning, the next grumble to Sonia and me that we are not pulling our weight in keeping the slope leaf- and weed-free, but these are good times. More often than not, she hides away for days, declining to answer her door, and feeling too reclusively poorly to speak should we ever see her outside.

No sign of her today, sadly. But here we are, because within a few steps we have reached our gates. Made of iron, they require a good scrub annually in mid-summer to remove the green algae that accumulates through the rainy season, *tsuyu*, which arrives less reliably these days due to climate change. It's a hell of a job. Mostly it's me who does it, but last year, because I was not here, Akii took on the task, and was shocked by how long it took, how fiddly the work involved . . .

The name on the gate is Akii's own: Ueda Yasuyuki, in the ideographic characters of Chinese origin known as *kanji*. Ueda is his family name, meaning upper rice paddy or field. Yasuyuki reads as safety. (Akii? A nickname from his childhood.)

My name is not there, simply because I am unfazed, unbothered. I am comfortable in my skin and that is all that matters. The post

office knows me, as do the officials in the *kohban*, or police box, in front of the train station. Though feminist in the true sense of expecting, and when needs be seeking if not demanding, equality, I no longer feel the need to make any song and dance about it.

Anyway, I don't really 'live' here, do I? I'm just passing through . . . my anthem of the last twenty-five years.

Walls of breeze-block line

the driveway. To the left it is topped with green wire netting, and creeper. On the right (higher) I have terracotta pots and, in the summer, greenery.

These vessels came from Sandra, a long-term American resident who lives nearby. She'd had enough of pot plants, she told me, wanting to cut down her workload — and with a Japanese mother-in-law in her nineties with dementia, and a mentally disabled sister-in-law who comes for the weekend at least once a month, who could blame her?

"Take as many as you like," she said, generous and kind far beyond the call of neighbourly duty.

The wall on the left ends in a garden. That on the right gives way to a bed of shrubs, behind which rises a high concrete wall, on the top of which nice neighbours, the Tanaka family, have their own home. He is a company man about to retire; his wife speaks good English; there is a son who moved to Tokyo, and a daughter who, having completed her education in the US, is currently working as an intern dolphin trainer in Hawaii.

Ugly degraded concrete continues around the back of their home also. All around this top end of our own small upland valley, in fact. It was bearable while vegetation softened the effect. But in 2008, men arrived and knocked down two unoccupied houses just above and beyond our own.

More real estate minions then proceeded to hack down all the old trees, including the plum that had hung over the driveway and starred our spring with white. They also destroyed camellias, pink and red, and a magnificent white magnolia, and finally sawed an ancient Virginia creeper through at the base. This meant that vines that had over the years spread over walls and roofs, turning the valley into a mini-paradise, withered on the stem.

After what had happened to us in Hayama, it was like a second death. Looking down now into the spaces left clean by the real

estate company chain Century 21— for neither plot has sold, and so are being reclaimed by what are euphemistically called weeds ("plants in the wrong place at the wrong time") — I still wonder at a culture that professes to love and respect nature, and yet is ready without compulsion to destroy for commercial interests.

Why does a plot have to be *kirei,* 'clean' or 'fresh'? When did this notion creep into accepted practices? All major changes — both cultural and economic — seem to go back to the post-war period. But I suspect it is later than that, maybe dating from the oil shock of the 1970s, or even the far more recent economic bubble of the late 1980s, when fear and greed once again turned the country's values upside down and inside out.

Asano-san says she and her family used to be able to step out of their second floor onto a metal bridge (still there) across to the hillside, and go hiking. But then even they succumbed to the fear-mongering propagated by the construction industry — that all mountains are inherently dangerous — to use the huge numbers of men taken off the land in the post-war period to rebuild the country in America's image, and keep them in employment. So, more concrete.

Read Alex Kerr's *Dogs and Demons – Tales from the Dark Side of Japan* for the inside story, as relevant today as when first published in 2001. Alex does as fine a journalistic job at getting at the truth as it is possible to accomplish without getting a right-wing-aimed bullet in the back for his trouble.

Apologies. I did not intend to become quite so emotional, but Concrete Unlimited has this effect on me. Once a country with one of the most beautiful coastlines in the world, something like eighty per cent is now affected to a ruinous degree — 'protected' according to government ordinance — by tetrapods. In addition, unfinished roads go nowhere. Bridges end mid-structure. Buildings go higher and higher, as if there is no earth-shaking tomorrow and the chaos theory is regarded simply as some nuthead's fantasy.

Even without the fifty-six nuclear power reactors that convenience deems necessary so as to keep lights on all night in golf practice ranges, vending machines operating twenty-four hours a day, and encouraging architects to design office buildings with no windows, it is all quite mad.

The only safe thing to say? Japan will surely rue the day.

All four of our homes since 1986,when the government began a scheme by which "Bubble" money was handed on a plate to every city, town and village to spend on signature expansion, have suffered from so-called development.

The lovely little teahouse we lived in from 1988–1990 is no more. That was in the Valley-of-the Fan (Ogigayatsu) in Kamakura, where the temple bell of Kaizo-ji woke us every morning at 6am and welcomed nightfall twelve hours later.

Our immediate neighbour, a carpenter who lived with his wife and father, was an orchid enthusiast, hanging pots from bamboo poles all over the garden in summer. Another habit we've adopted, though our poles are less exotic; his own created a breeze-fluttering butterfly-like flower collection without compare — utterly ravishing.

Now everything has gone, and a bright yellow two-floor block of apartments stands on the site. Traditional architecture blends naturally into the landscape; now it wants to be noticed!

The only remnant of our lives that still holds its own in that once paradisiacal place? The cherry tree that I planted on the bank above the now long-deceased *obaachan,* an elderly woman who lived on the corner below in a crumbling wooden house with no running water, no heating, and a single bare light bulb.

She was as tough as they come, heading off to the *sentoh* or public bathhouse (also now gone) down in the town every evening, and feeding an army of stray cats that collected twice daily in timely tune with the ringing of the temple bell.

Happy times, and a home much loved by all who came to stay, even though on occasion we had to sleep head to toe to cram everyone in.

My daughter, Buffy, was an early visitor in 1989. En route back to London after a year-long working holiday in Australia, where she had met her Canadian husband-to- be, she came with me to the City Office in Chigasaki when Akii and I went to register our marriage.

Son Lee's best friend Paul was another guest; tired, and what he termed 'templed-out' by months of traveling in Asia, all he wanted was to be mothered, to have the many knots of cultural excitement and confusion and sheer muscular exhaustion unravelled with endless cups of tea.

Then there was Amanda, who called from Narita International Airport, northeast of Tokyo, explaining that her father was a friend of my ex-husband, and that she and her friend Marianne were on their way home from Mexico, had no money, and could they come to stay. The cheek was so outstanding that we put them up for a month and watched with a kind of appalled admiration as they took Japan by storm.

British comedian Bill Bailey was another who passed through. Well over two decades ago, he was honing his vast array of theatrical skills as a member of a small troupe of actors (Passe-Partout) taking Third World subjects like women's rights and HIV into Japanese and international schools. Wild Bill, of the strumming guitar and quiet but easy joke — and yes, even then he was having trouble with his hair.

Hayama? A two-floor wooden house up a steep flight of stone steps, again in traditional style. Passe-Partout stayed there also, but different faces, different names. Only the founders, Michelle and Dick, remained constant.

Florence from Nairobi, for example, with whom we exchanged *nengajoh* or end-of-year greeting cards until only a year or so ago, when silence fell. We do hope she and her family are alright. Kenya has not been a safe place in recent years.

Also Judi, Catherine, Isabel, Sandy, Sarah and Adrian, Andy and Joan, Ingrid and Freddie, Ingrid and Duncan, Lee . . . just a few of those from the UK who used our home as a base for travels or respite.

Louise and Fred from Australia. Buffy (moved to Toronto) and her husband Ross.

Plus all those friends of friends — and friends of friends of friends who passed through . . . what were their names, now, I struggle to recall?

Remember though the New Year we had four guys in the house, together with one of their mothers? Toshiko Hatta died in Fukushima last year, but her son is still in London, managing a hair salon in Mayfair. What fun that was, playing charades, dancing, drinking — a lot of drinking! — and visiting the local port to see all the fishing boats dressed up with celebratory bamboo and flags.

We have such a funny photo of you all, standing in a line waiting for the bus — Nik (now in Montreal), Alan (back in Wales), John (still in Tokyo), and Mamoru, with Toshiko-san, she half their size. She slept upstairs with us, on the other side of the papered *shohji* screens. The guys laid out in a row downstairs, head to toe, like sardines in a can, giggling fit to bust.

Today, seven years later, that address — 1234 Isshiki (yes, really) is used as a storehouse. As for all the trees and bamboo that surrounded it — levelled. I went back once to take a look, but never again. Better to simply retain the memories, for they at least can never be demolished, except by time. So now we are at 3-3-3 Yamanone — an equally memorable address.

And yes, you're right, I did miss one out: the fourth-floor apartment I lived in for two years after first arriving in Japan in April, 1986. That was in Chigasaki (down along the Shonan coast that stretches from Odawara on the southern edge of the Kanto plain, to Miura Hanto, the tiny peninsula on which we live now) and in Hamamidaira (a state-owned complex, *danchi*, like council housing) accommodating several thousand Japanese, and me.

After leaving my beautiful home in London's Queen's Park, it was a massive shock to the system, but rather than run back to the UK, my tail between my legs, I gritted my teeth and allowed it to become healing.

After years of working freelance in publishing, bringing up a family and all the responsibilities involved, it proved liberating to have no bills to pay, little to no cleaning to do, nothing to worry about but cycling to the coast and dancing on the boardwalk to Madonna or Talking Heads, and to take the bus or train up and down the coast, exploring. I had come to recover, recharge my batteries, change my life, and that is what I took time to accomplish.

The reason that Hamamidaira (roughly rather than literally

translated as 'a flat place from which to see the beach'), while to be respected, was never a place I came to love?

Built of concrete in the post-war era, and depressingly degraded, it is being knocked down even as I write, to be replaced with new updated blocks, but made of the same soul-and-fabric-destroying stuff. It doesn't last well, you see. The wind behind the salt air, the climate — freezing to tropical — wreaks havoc. Japan has a lot of very expensive problems looming on the horizon, when it all has to be renewed.

Which brings me to a small domestic case in point . . .

THE CAVE

horaana

We don't make use of this hole-in-the wall as much as we used to, simply because the concrete above the entrance to our cave is so decomposed, and the supporting beam so rusted, that we live in genuine fear of the whole thing crashing about our ears.

But still, we have a cave — our very own cave. Presumably, it was excavated from the hillside behind to act as a storehouse for outside stuff, and that is exactly what we use it for: bikes, including the beloved ageing heirloom Brenda, named after the Australian friend from whom I purchased it when she returned to Melbourne in 2006 after a decade in Japan.

Also gardening equipment, ladders and lengths of bamboo, plus all manner of bits and bobs: the top and legs of a table I used to write on; buckets and spades for digging labyrinths on the beach

— you walk them to find answers, not to get even more lost; bags and bags of bits of blue and white china, picked up from the sand (where will the mosaic be, that I am supposed to create from this detritus? oh for a definitive answer so I could get on with it); and yes, next to the beehive, a large, mouldering packing case.

We really should throw this out, but Glen and Michael are coming back from the UK to visit this summer, and you never know your luck, they may want to take the various belongings that they left behind four years ago when they removed themselves to Birmingham.

Roberto had worked so hard too. A Japanese-Brazilian carpenter, he had made the box to accommodate a very lovely *tansu* (chest of drawers/cupboard for storage), the glass panels of which had already gone ahead, so to speak. But at the last minute, Glen realized the box was too big to meet the required measurements of Customs, so he wrenched off the top in a fury, moved the tansu into our house (we not being there at the time to argue otherwise), and flung the box in the furthest corner of the cave.

There is a lesson here, of course; there always is, but at the time, no-one would be told!

Our poor cave tends to be at the receiving end of such mini-dramas. It's bloody useful, though. Happiest, however, when small children stand at the entrance in mock terror and shout: hellooooooo. Or rather (being mostly Japanese): *harrooooooo*. Which is quite amusing really because the word in the Japanese language (*nihongo*), for such a hole in the wall is *hora-ana*!

I'm exaggerating, of course.

It's not that scary. Nor very big.

But it is a cave.

THE ENTRANCE HALL, INSIDE AND OUT
genkan

Broad and deep and protected from the rain by a green copper-clad roof, our entrance and hallway offer a welcoming oasis of calm. To the left of the sliding doors of glass and wood, stands a small stone-carved Edo-period statue of a Buddhist priest, shaded by a scented lemon geranium; in the corner, a Bizen pot stands crammed full of umbrellas. This I rescued from former landlady Tabei-san's possessions when everything was being thrown out next door as *sodai gomi* (big rubbish or, in slang terminology, unwanted husbands!) after her death in Hayama in the late 1990s.

Which reminds me: it is time to put out a round flat dish full of water, in which blossoms, petals or leaves collected from the garden through spring into autumn find solace. A custom picked up in Okinawa many years ago, it always provides enormous pleasure. Today, I choose a natural stoneware plate, a red camellia floating . . .

To the right of the doorway, set atop a somewhat grubby white plastic garden shelf unit, is a somewhat surreal torso! A Japanese form-fitting fashion mannequin, much battered and wreathed with a circlet of twigs and berries, and a large green satin bow — remnants of a Christmas past, and to which I add a red ribbon every December 21st to mark the shortest day and help relieve the gloom of mid-winter.

What else? Lots more blue and white bits . . . a nicely slipped vase found on a demolition site . . . a large battle-sized horseshoe (designed for sturdiness, not for speed) . . . lumps of bleached dead coral, innumerable shells . . . smooth ocean-rounded Birthing Stones . . . pieces of wood twisted by tide and tangle — all manner of jetsom and flotsam. I'm a passionate beachcomber.

On the wall above hangs a small, naturally shaped wooden plaque — another find — with the letters of our names glued on, but back to front, so that you could use it as a stencil. Now where did I find them — the mirror image of the letters for Angela & Akii.

As of late, Angela Aki is the name of a Japanese-American double-culture singer-pianist with a large cult following and much admired. It creates much confusion, a lot of amusement.

＊ ＊ ＊

So, welcome. *Irasshaimase. Dohzo yoroshiku.* Please step inside.

In summer, we install a screen so that one of the sliding glass doors can remain open while barring entry to the armies of mosquitoes that seek to invade from June through to October. In this way, the outside becomes the inside and vice versa, but without the buzzing intrusion.

Time then to take off shoes, feel the cool of massaging pebbles

set between tiles, and step up into the interior of the *genkan*. There are waist-high built-in cupboards right and left for storing winter shoes in summer, summer shoes in winter. For now, though, simply leave your shoes right here, below the step, toes turned towards the door so you can slip into them easily when you leave. No problem if you forget; I will do it for you, quietly, so you do not notice.

Service — the Japanese way.

Ignore the wall coverings, which bizarrely mock brickwork below and a greenish hessian above. (I always meant to cover up the bricks with rattan, but have to date never got around to it.)

Instead, with or without the slippers provided, tread softly on the rather nice but well-worn Persian carpet, for hereby hangs a tale . . .

It began with an introduction around year 2000 to two American women, a couple. Two years later, with no contact in-between, the more masterful of the two called to ask a favour: would Akii act as a sponsor for an apartment she wanted to rent in Tokyo? Her partner had cancer and was in Hiro-o hospital; she needed to be closer. Akii, being the kind trusting soul he is, said yes, of course, and did the deed.

Eighteen months later, again with no contact — not even a thank you which, when I think about it, ought maybe to have rung alarm bells — the real estater who had found them the apartment called us. Where were they? With bills to the ceiling and no rent paid for months, Akii's kindness (naivety, we now began to fear) was called to the bar.

For my part, I felt wholly responsible. It was I who had asked him to help them, so it was my fault, not his. Culturally this is how it works in Japan.

Anyway, when entry was gained, the partner — sick or otherwise — was found hiding in the back bedroom (and the next day disappeared). But of Ms Masterful, there was no sign.

In accordance with the landlord's wishes, the apartment was emptied and we spent a very unhappy week or more in a back room at the real estater's office, listing all the contents and taking photos, just in case either woman returned and decided to cry, "thief!"

The furniture and electrical goods, as it turned out, were valueless. Clothes went to the Salvation Army. But even I could not throw out what I knew to be Ms M.'s personal belongings, items she had once described with great emotion and affection: her mother's china and linen, photo albums, letters. So I boxed them up and sent them for what may well be perpetual storage with the Japan Help Line.

We took only a few things in lieu of all the bills paid: some cushions, which I quickly gave up on as having bad energy — Glen had no such misgivings, so they were passed on — and the rug.

For a year or so we got some pleasure from stepping on it. But then Ms M. caught up with me, or rather I with her. Discovered (through the auspices of the American Embassy) hanging out on one of the Balearic Islands in the Mediterranean, she professed total ignorance of the trouble she had left behind.

By this time, through discussions with her lawyer in Alabama, I had learned she was in fact a very wealthy woman who had made her way around Asia for several years behaving in much the same way: nesting and then upping and offing, leaving messes behind for others to clear up. Trouble was, he and the Court had to obey her deceased parents' wishes according to their will, and ensure there was money enough to last her lifetime. This meant debts could not/would not be paid.

She was sick, Ms M. bleated plaintively. How could I bother her with such trivialities? When I replied that what might be trivial to her was most certainly not to those who worked hard to make an honest living, I received back a fax with a single line: *Die in the name of Christ.*

This was when I realized just how ill she was, and began treading more softly.

Our tabby cat, Tora (meaning tiger), however, remains oblivious, and sharpens her claws on all four corners of the rug. For the time being at least, we let her get on with it.

For balance, happier stuff...

On top of the left-hand shoe cupboard, a huge square blue and white Imari plate, bought as a wedding present by the company of Japanese women, TGA Inc., that I worked for between 1989 and 1994, helping establish, edit and write for their client magazine.

Also a whale, carved from a fragment of ebony picked up from the semi-tropical forest floor, a one-off created by a local craftsman on the largest of the Bonin Islands, Ogasawara, one thousand kilometres south of Tokyo, yet under the jurisdiction of the metropolis. We travelled there by ferry — a twenty-six-hour journey — in 1992. All these years later and still no airstrip, hotels or golf courses: praise be.

Alongside, a hand-made washi paper lamp made by Shoi and Colleen, artists who live down the coast in Akiya. I light the candle inside on special occasions, so that the kanji character reading *shizuka/sei*, for quiet serenity, gleams warmly through the dark and sets the tone.

On the wall above hangs a photo of Akii and me walking in the early 1990s through paddy fields in Yamanashi, the foothills of Mt. Fuji. We had gone there with Tateo and Hiroki, then married and living in a tiny flat hanging off the hillside in Hayama, overlooking the ocean.

The purpose was hugely optimistic but, as we soon realized, wildly unrealistic: we wanted to find out if we could hack out a living there, taking over one or more of the many cherry orchards that were falling into disuse as farmers died and their children no longer wanted to get their hands dirty.

The average life-span of farmers in Japan is now seventy and, while still failing to impinge on the consciousness of the Japanese public, on whom it will undoubtedly have the worst affect, there is great anxiety among agriculturalists and associated government officials: who will grow Japan's food in the future?

As it turned out, I — the foreigner — was the only one ready and willing to give it a try. The others — our friends in particular — realized they were too used to their creature comforts, and the demand to conform to rural life was just too tough. More likely I would be forgiven cultural indiscretions, being an outsider (*gaikokujin,* or *gaijin* for short) who could not possibly understand The Japanese Way; it would be they as *nihonjin* (Japanese people) who would most likely have had the hardest time fitting into a tight-knit traditional community.

But back now to our second tight-fitting traditional shoe cupboard, this time to the right, below a small window and topped with a ceramic lion from Okinawa. Usually people buy a pair, to sit on roofs or gateposts, to protect the house from bad spirits, but I could only afford — and carry! — one.

Plus another of Colleen and Shoi's lamps, a farewell *sayounara* gift from George (now retired in Florida but at that point in time off to Eastern Europe) and swiftly nicknamed 'The Washington Monument'.

Also, a two-tier blue and white round ceramic box that echoes a larger one in fine woven rattan, situated on the other side of the entranceway.

An emu egg in a glass-fronted box (another rubbish heap *gomi* find in Hayama with its own — no doubt — extraordinary story), now sitting atop a pile of little cushions made by yours truly from scraps of cotton *kasuri* (Japan's traditional form of ikat dyeing and weaving), stitched and tasselled with red silk.

A turned wooden bowl from Australia brimming with bean pods and bits and bobs.

And a four-sided black lacquer vase filled with feathers, mostly crow and kite feathers picked up from round about because both birds are deemed messengers in ancient myths and legends.

I believe in signs, you see.

It was a sign that took me to an RBR-organised workshop facilitated by Dr. Betty Edwards in 1999 (she of the bestselling book *Drawing on the Right Side of the Brain).*

After an interview, she invited me to participate, to which I heard myself reply, "Well, that is kind, but no, it's impossible. I'm far too busy." But part of me wanted to go, so the night before I threw the decision to fate: if I woke in time to catch the train for the required 10am start in Tokyo, I would go. If not, well that would be that. Would you believe it: I was awake at 5am.

The self-portrait drawn — or rather rubbed out from a charcoal base for light and shadow — accomplished on the last day of the five-day course, hangs on one wall. For years after, passing by this mirror-image always made me shake my head: why so tough on myself? Why so self-critical? Assessment in any shape or form would be different now.

Akii's drawing hangs on the other wall, opposite. It took him seven years to decide to do the course, this time run by Kristin, also from California but with Icelandic blood, and it was even more wildly successful than before.

I remember him returning after his first day, standing in the genkan, holding out a drawing he had done of his hand:

"I didn't know I could do anything like this. . . " he said, tears in his eyes.

This from the man who, on our first meeting in London, in 1984, had dismissed his own gifts, saying that he was a rationalist and not at all creative.

A turning point in so many ways.

Now when people marvel at his self-portrait, they remark on how it reflects the patient, loving, gentle and wonderfully creative man he truly is.

Thank you, Kristin.

Admiration also for Kiki — a professional wrestler turned artist in Japan whose belief in herself left me at that time speechless with envy; her small canvas of Richmond's Kew Gardens, in dollops of orange, green and pink oil paints, hangs just around the corner by the small window.

I have no doubt she has reinvented herself all over again with equal measures of confidence back in her native Germany, or wherever she is now. Aachen actually; I just looked her up, and now we are reunited, via Facebook.

A deep, loving respect to Liga, recently moved back to California from her studio-home in Hayama to be closer to her grandchildren.

A Chinese-American, whose father sponsored the first pioneering gateway into Yokohama's Chinatown, she is an artist of true and remarkable talent. The little watercolour of winter narcissus that she gave me one spring now sits in a narrow bamboo frame. Her large painterly canvases are a different story: replete with symbols and images that pull us into a dreamlike world of psychological angst. Much missed. (You, Liga, not the angst.)

And gratitude to the owner of Folk Art Gallery, who in 2003 when I stumbled into her wonderful emporium of furniture and collectables from Korea and China, had premises in Tokyo's Ebisu district, but has since retrenched in harder times to her original address in Shibuya.

Hiroko's story made for a great article, and I often dropped in after that. Remarking one day on the particular merits of a piece of antique Chinese embroidery, you could have knocked me down with one of my feathers when it turned up the following week by *takkyubin* (Japan's wonderful 24-hour delivery service), with a thank you note.

I can count on one hand the gifts received as thanks for articles written over the twenty-two years I conducted weekly interviews for The Japan Times (from 1987 to 2008). It was not a custom I normally encouraged, or approved of. But this was something I accepted with unadulterated joy, and had framed accordingly, in Chinese style: black lacquer, rounded corners.

It looks very fine, hanging on the wall facing the entrance way, between a small round copper circle punched with holes, and the very first artefact I ever purchased in Japan: an old painted and lacquered wooden shop sign, carved with the two *hiragana* characters for *ame* (sweet or sweets; there are no plurals in the Japanese language).

Hiragana is one of Japan's two written phonetic alphabets, in this case created by women who from the eighth century were not allowed to study or employ imported Chinese ideographs. This is one explanation, anyway; there are others.

Below, on a small battered black *tansu* (most probably once part of a much larger piece of furniture, and bought from Milk Hall in Kamakura), stands a square glass container of bamboo twigs, hung with a marker woven by a local artist. Sachiko collects all the materials for her weaving from the hillsides round about, then strips out the fibres and softens them for working into beautiful interior textiles.

It makes you ponder on what Japanese used to wear, when there was no native cotton or wool, and silk was elitist. The answer lies in whatever they were able to weave to make pliable fabrics, and amazingly this included lichens, moss and seaweed. In Hokkaido, Japan's northernmost populated island, indigenous Ainu manipulated bark as well as bear skins. All a long time ago, of course, but still . . . weaving flax and grasses is a craft tradition that continues.

There are fresh flowers always, standing on the small black *kaidan* (staircase) picked up last year in the local citizens' flea market and hard to resist at 300 yen. From the tribal figures carved in its wooden surface, I should imagine it to be from Bali, or somewhere in Indonesia. They are jolly dancing gods, and make the genkan an even happier place. Aided and abetted by fresh water and the various circular objects described, so meeting all the basic criteria of positively-energised Chinese principles of feng shui, known in Japanese as *fuu sui*/wind and water (of which more later) for an entrance hall.

Whatever works, I say.

THE TOILET
washiki no toire

The part-tiled *toire,* as pronounced in Japanese and indeed Japanese in style, is off the *genkan* entrance hall, in the far right-hand corner, its door directly opposite to that leading into Akii's room.

Inside there is the requisite pair of toilet slippers, a washbasin and mirror below a small window out to the back, and two more doors. That to the right leads into the men's standing urinal, the only decoration being a shaped wooden beam leaning against the wall in the corner. (Furthest away from the pee-box, so that it does not get sprayed on.)

Joseph carried back this lovely but very heavy piece of wood for me on his shoulder many years ago, after we had rescued several items from a house being demolished. Where is he now, I wonder?

Last heard of in Boston, at a Buddhist seminary, studying *The Tibetan Book of the Dead* to assist AIDS patients with dying rites, I remember an especially riotous New Year party in his exquisite little traditional house in a bamboo grove up a steep hillside in Kita-Kamakura.

When he left, he gave me a book, inscribed, "This is a bequest, with love, 8-18-93." (August 18 1993.) Little wonder that now *The Great Age of Chinese Poetry, The High T'ang,* by Stephen Owen, has pride of place on my poetry shelf.

By contrast — though when I think about it, (in accordance with deep-rooted Confucian tradition), in this country, customarily women have to be lower than men in just about everything they do — the female toilet is squat in design. Many hate sinking so low, while others love it, thinking it far more natural than sitting on a seat.

Sadly, I have no choice. My knees no longer bend.

There is a wooden piece of décor in here too: an old sign for an *ikebana* flower arranging school. Again it's nothing special, but I just hate to see anything intrinsically interesting and lovely go to waste.

Which is why, below the washbasin, looking forlorn and out of sorts, a collage of African village life created from straw and wood leans against the wall. I found it thrown away on our local rubbish heap just last year, and thought, 'Well, someone will love it.'

So here I am, and here it is: an English agent for salvage requiring recycling, and an African community awaiting recognition and rescue.

AKII'S ROOM
Akii no heya

The notices on the door say it all. One shows a picture of a small Japanese man kneeling on a flat *zabuton* cushion telling a story, a traditional theatrical form known as *rakugo*. The other offers a disarrayed cat with a message in English: MY STUFF, MY MESS, MY BUSINESS.

To be fair, Akii's room is pretty tidy these days, but it's not so clean. Mostly because Tora-chan loves to sit on his huge pale-blue-painted desk, or his colourful patchwork quilt, or the zabuton upon which he rehearses his rakugo stories, or the much-faded handwoven silk, triangular Thai fold-up mattress, should it be lying open on the floor. Lots of fur! Rika, who comes in for a couple of hours every two weeks to vacuum and whisk a duster around, steers clear. So do I, otherwise I get accused of behaving like his mother.

35

Not quite knowing where to start, I ask him what he would save if there were a fire. Maybe I could write about these choices? But his reply is typical:

Initially he thought he would grab his computer . . . then the photograph of his great-grandfather at dental university taken in the Meiji period (1868-1912) . . . or maybe the small silver-painted relief of Pegasus made by his younger brother Yasumasa, who committed suicide in 1978.

But then Akii changed his mind.

Nothing, he decided. It would have to be everything or nothing. So . . . nothing.

Not the telescope nor the ukulele, because although given as gifts (by guess whom), he felt no attachment because he'd never made use of them. Nor the shelf of photograph albums containing the evidence of our lives together (one for each year from 1987 to 2005, when we went digital); far too heavy.

Not one of the hundreds of books that fill cupboards and line other shelves. Not one of the many records — singles and albums — that sit in piles or stand stacked beside his vintage music system. Nor even any of the remembrances of his childhood — a painted metal train carriage, a basket full of marbles. Student years: a mah-jong set (which he is using to teach our young neighbour Julia how to play, but mostly she just loves the swooshing sound the tiles make in action). Anything related to his working life? Nothing to write home about, he says, wittily; a waste of time.

Then there are the rabbits. Being born in 1951 makes him a rabbit according to the traditional Chinese calendar, so there are a few around.

Also bees, but these are a more recent interest, and why I bought the plate from Jill at her last biannual exhibition in Shinjuku's Keio Department Store, to hang on his wall as an anniversary gift. Stoneware, painted with butterflies, it conjures up memories of our time in Kamakura; the tulips are a favourite flower; and as for the merrily buzzing nectar and pollen gatherers, well, Akii recently ordered his first hive from a beekeeper in Kawasaki, and is making preparations.

Already he is thinking of designing a label for jars of *Yamanone Hachimitsu* (Yamanone Honey), taking orders even. They will be Japanese bees, by the way, not the European variety so badly hit by a viral attack in 2008. Called *nihon mitsubachi* (*Apis cerana japonica*), the native variety is smaller, darker and, while relatively gentle, decidedly more maverick in temperament; they tend to do their own thing, flying off at a moment's notice, taking to the mountains like the wild, untameable creatures they really are.

After quitting his job in Tokyo in May 2009 simply for the sake of retaining his sanity, Akii spent that summer visiting beekeepers in Kyoto, and at his cousin's temple in relatively nearby Wakayama Prefecture, and attending workshops in Nagano Prefecture (on the west side of the Japan Alps) and Ginza, bang in the heart of Tokyo and where — amazingly — many urban enthusiasts tend hives on the tops of buildings.

He also spent ten days in silence at a Vipassana meditation retreat outside Kyoto. That he completed a task that for many would be sheer torture, did not surprise me. Yes, he is on the surface immensely patient, stoic and heroic, but believing himself to be the opposite, he has made obstinacy — or rather the armour of obstinacy — his second name.

So how to persuade the man — now sitting at his desk, trailing through Mixi, a Japanese social networking site — to talk more about his room, and maybe even get rid of a few things? He's pretty involved, mailing and chatting away with beekeepers up and down the country, but I can but try.

I could perhaps use a de-cluttering technique once introduced by a student writer, which she reckoned saved her life as a hardworking housewife and mother and gave her time to do Other Things (like writing). It's from the website *FlyLady.net* And while I found the whole concept slightly appalling, I quite often find myself cleaning the sink nightly before going to bed, as instructed, to give the morning start the illusion of being that much brighter and better organised.

Anyway, I give him a plastic bag and ask him to walk around and drop in at random a dozen items that he has no use for. (Another FlyLady tip; an easy regular way to get rid of stuff, to simplify.) Items arbitrarily picked from around the room as follows:

* one fist-sized dirty yellow rubber brain, with *Drawing on the Right Side of the Brain* printed on the base
* a grungy black wool pull-on hat (holey)
* National socket (?)
* Mitsubishi remote control (for what?)
* one over-sized glove (whose?)
* small red plastic mail or post box still in wrapper (*hanko* signature seal case)
* mini book for herbs (keep it)
* mini book — *Red Directory (The Sushi Menu)* in English, Francais, Deutsch, Italiano, Espanol, Portugais — again, keep it!
* mini atlas (very out of date)
* ceramic pig (bell)
* tube of pearl toothpaste (unopened but way beyond sell-by date)
* rakugo performance donation coffer recycled creatively from detergent box, sides pasted with cut-out illustrations of good luck symbols, *yen* signs, pirates' loot, etc. Top designed like a suggestive pair of open lips . . . (shades of The Rolling Stones' cover of *Sticky Fingers*). Don't need it any more, apparently, not now that we don't have to collect

donations to pay *sensei* — the rakugo teacher with whom Akii studied for several years — for showing his face down here at related events.

Yet still I don't feel I am doing his room justice, because while shambolic and dusty, it is who he is, and yet he is neither of these things. I spent months over the summer wondering how to get a handle on it, on him.

And then I realized why I was so stuck: because he was stuck, professionally and personally. Trying to reinvent himself as a translator was proving tough in the current economic market.

Also, his father was dying.

Now in mid-autumn, his father has passed on, so maybe we can move on.

I try another tack, inspired by reading an old copy of *Granta*, the English magazine that publishes new writing. In the issue FOOD, published in 1995, Georges Perec (1936–1982) attempted an inventory of all the food he had eaten in the year 1974.

It begins, *Nine beef broths, one iced-cucumber soup, one mussel soup . . .* closes with *N* (sic) *coffees, one tisane, three Vichy waters.* While in-between, six pages of itemizing, from which my favourite (simply for the sound of it) may be, *One bilberry Kugelhupf.*

So I could do this, list everything in Akii's room, music, for example: X number of CDs, tapes, 33rmp vinyl albums, single 45s . . .

Asked which piece of music was the most precious to him, Akii knew exactly where to go for the sample album, *Cobalt Hours*, by Yuming (Yumi Matsutoya). It had belonged to his younger brother — Yasumasa's own most precious possession — for inside was a photo of the famed Japanese singer-songwriter in her younger days, and written on the back in his own writing, Yoyogi Park 1975.

Yasumasa must have been at the concert in central Tokyo, Akii realises.

His most prized books are four comic *manga* from the 1950s, when he was a small boy growing up in post-war Japan.

"They're pretty battered and wouldn't fetch much in the market," he continues, "but whenever I have them in my hands and open them, I feel a thrill." His favourite? *Igaguri-Kun,* from 1957, about a small boy who loves judo. (Akii would have been six.)

As he began sifting through the shelves, looking for more

treasures, I suddenly thought, 'Good god, am I mad? Life's too short; I've got X number of rooms still to go, a book to write. Get on with it, woman.'

As I turn to leave, nearly skating to an early death on the brightly coloured woven rug he had carried back from Mexico in 2006 (he loves yellow, as sunny as it comes), I see the only thing that I personally might grab in an emergency: the framed photograph of Akii with Charlie, taken soon after I had introduced them in my kitchen in London's Queen's Park in 1985.

Charlie Charles was one of the original Blockheads, the drummer in Ian Drury's band, one of the founders of the UK punk music scene in the 1970s. It is Charlie's tight musicianship you hear on the outrageously direct 1979 No. 1 in the UK charts, *Hit me with your rhythm stick, hit me, hit me!* — a double entendre, par excellence.

Born in British Guiana, now Guyana, in South America, Charlie was open, kindly and generous — again, almost to a fault. He was also a brilliant drummer. Though much loved and respected, I suspect it was this sweetly naive vulnerability that worked against his ever making big bucks or getting the songs that poured out of him into print and onto vinyl.

He and I had got to know one another in the early 1980s as committee members of KiSAC, trying to save the historic State Cinema on London's Kilburn High Road from demolition, for use as a multi-cultural arts centre.

Ironically, but perhaps not un-coincidentally, Ian Drury and The Blockheads began life as Kilburn & the High Roads, because that was where he too lived in 1970.

It was a tough time from 1982 through to 1985 and Charlie proved the very best of friends — always there when needed, always the perfect gentleman, the truest of gentle men. We kept in touch after I moved to Japan, and it was on one of my return visits that he died.

It was clear from my first visit to his hospital bedside that the cancer was moving fast, but I was not to know just how swiftly and relentlessly. I remember walking through central London's Soho district and stopping in front of a Japanese restaurant: Charlie had asked for sushi but I was on my way to Scotland for my mother's eightieth birthday and a family reunion; did I have time or not?

It was while driving back down south with Akii, Buffy and Ross a week or so later that his death was announced over the radio. Apparently I was inconsolable, obsessed with the fact that I had not found the time to take him the one thing he had asked of me: sushi.

Though I am sure I have been long forgiven, it still haunts me to a degree, acting as an important lesson: to try not to put off today what might not be possible tomorrow.

So, there is Charlie, hiding behind sunglasses and under a halo of dreadlocks, hugely grinning. And Akii — they have their arms around each other, looking pleased as punch to see one another again; so shockingly young, both of them, a state in which Charlie is now frozen forever in time for me.

Akii was even happier when Charlie visited Tokyo (one of several trips through the late 1980s) to back his old friend Kiyoshiroh (also now passed on from cancer). Kiyoshiroh Imawano (born Kiyoshiroh Kurihara) was not only the leader and vocalist of the ground-breaking band RC Succession, but a rebel with a cause; he was passionately — fiercely — anti-nuclear.

After one gig in Shibuya, we got hauled off with Charlie to the band's favourite *izakaya* (pub) and Akii was able to rub shoulders with one of Japan's most maverick stars. To some Kiyoshiroh was a rock-and-roller, to others he was a folk singer and political activist; those in the business simply thought of him as a musician's musician.

Just like Charlie.

Having just read this through, and laughing quite a lot, Akii notes that the photo was not taken in my kitchen (though this was where he and Charlie first met), but rather at Deirdre's house in Notting Hill.

"At that reunion party in London in 1987, after my first visit to Scotland to meet your mother and aunt," he reminisces fondly. "Remember?"

I do.

Or, rather, I do now.

THE CORRIDOR
rohka

Take no notice of the grinning tribal mask above the doorway, though it is a bit freaky when one of its teeth falls out. Overall it is a protective spirit, so it's not surprising perhaps that many visitors say it is the one thing they would like to take away with them. Nothing in this house has ever disappeared or gone walkabout, however.

Unlike in London, where in 1981 at my fortieth birthday party — a foolish kind of bash, I realised long ago, designed as much to prove to myself how many friends I had at the time as provide a fun time for all — a small drawing of great sentimental value went missing from the toilet. I'm still wondering which of my imagined one hundred and twenty best friends decided to relieve me of it!

Luckily, the small band of intimates of old I am left with in the UK after twenty-four years being mostly out of sight if not mind are the salt of the earth, with whom I'd trust my very life.

You all know who you are.

A strip blanket hung from a bamboo pole divides the *genkan* from the corridor itself. Bought in Banaue in the Philippines, it is woven in stripes of varying width in red and black acrylic fibre because that is what Catholic nuns and priests were pressing local tribes to use in 1988, when I visited, rather than their traditional fibres and natural colouring agents. That overworked word again: convenience.

The Philippines is a collection of some seven thousand islands, with two major landmasses, Luzon to the north (predominantly Roman Catholic) and Muslim Mindanao to the south. (I was exploring northern Luzon in 1987, a long time ago now, to write a travel story for a literary magazine as was called, well, *The Magazine*.)

Back in 1966, when rationalization took off, there were hundreds of tribes in the Ifugao region around Lagawe, and many were head-hunters (the subject of my story). Needless to say, the Church was as unhappy with the custom as those who lost their heads, and implemented change. Typically, the men took to drink (while the rice grew) and the women kept on creating: having babies, cooking and weaving.

But while the raw materials for their craft were manufactured and imported from the city, the strap looms remained in use, which is how I came to buy a piece that perfectly illustrated Ancient and Modern in combination. For sure it is easy to care for — a quick but gentle turn in the washing machine and it comes up like new.

But is that everything?

In winter it is drawn against the draughts that are part and parcel of living in an Old(ish) Japanese House; in summer it is knotted and hangs out of the way. When she was small, Julia liked to swing on it, but at near-on eight she is now too grown up, and simply gives it a friendly pat as she passes through.

She pats a lot of things in the house, familiars all.

The corridor itself stretches ahead, floored with shining planks and an old but perfectly respectable oval rug of black rags speckled with white. I bought several of these at the same time from the same household shop in Kamakura; the smallest in the bathroom, the other upstairs.

To the left, a picture — the only artwork in this part of the house — a narrow vertical traditional watercolour, purchased somewhere en route between Beijing, Xian, Shanghai and Nanjing in 1993.

Then papered sliding doors into the living area. Not in a good state of repair, I have to admit; here bashed, there ripped . . . the downside to being opposite the storeroom, with stuff constantly being moved in and out, and having a cat with claws.

Lastly, on the left, an unlikely (some say) lamp hung high: slotted pieces of white plastic (from the Tokyu Hands store in Shibuya), which casts a contemporary light among ancestral shadows.

I like that.

On the right is first a cupboard for hanging coats, and then two sliding doors, all made in the same wood. The stairs to the second floor (what would be the first floor in some Western countries) are directly after. Then a broom cupboard.

All this wood normally requires little care, but during the early-summer rainy season displays a mind of its own, when mould grows on anything organic: wood acquires a white veil of bacteria; leather shoes turn green.

Are the coats of any interest?

Maybe the heavy reversible Thai jacket bought in a boutique in Meguro in the heady days of Japan's economic bubble when, for the first time in my life, I had what felt like disposable income in my pockets. One side is dyed blue-black with appliquéd patches of antique embroidery, including a baby's carrying sling stitched flat on to the back. The reverse side is *aizome* (a form of ikat, dyed with indigo on white cotton) stitched with zigzag bands of red ribbon and embroidered in yellow and scarlet cross- stitch.

Which side do I mostly wear? Depends on my mood.

And the brooms?

The most recent acquisition was purchased just last year, from an elderly woman in her eighties, up from the country, who came to the door with a bundle strapped to her back. Sitting on the step of the genkan, which is traditionally where trading is done, she told me the names of each style, and explained how the grasses had been woven and bundled together.

With each a work of art, it was impossible not to fall in love and part with far more money than I could afford at the time. But the *obaachan* went away happy and now, when I open the door of the cupboard to pull out the vacuum cleaner, and see her handiwork hanging on its own special hook, and know that she went away to create another to fill the gap in her wares, there is great satisfaction.

'Satisfaction in the creation of a broom?' many may be thinking. Well, how weird is that! Has the woman gone mad?

It makes me happy to think so.

Better to be crazy than normal, whatever crazy or normal are.

STORE ROOM NO. 1
hitotsume no nando

This first of four hidey holes (or dumping grounds) is not a pretty sight. It was not renewed for our tenancy, so *fusuma* were torn and grubby when we moved in, let alone now. But, as with the cave, it is immensely useful. When showing visitors around, I open the door dramatically and announce it as, The Ironing Room.

There are often shrieks of disbelief, especially from the Japanese: You have an ironing room? This is the size of my whole apartment! (Or at least the size of the living room or bedroom.)

Eyes then focus in wandering fashion on the three large masks, to the left and right of, and above the window, found in a junk shop soon after arriving in Chigasaki.

Then, being Alice-in-Wonderland in Japan, I found them mysterious, theatrical, amazing. Now they are simply increasingly battered old friends who accompany us on our travels. Ancient caricatured images of a couple: the white female mask is Okame, the man with a funny self-mocking face, Hyottoko.

The red mask with a long phallic nose (which always provokes amusement) is Tengu (literally Celestial Dog), a mythological creature whose origins are lost in Hindu/Buddhist/Shinto religious and animist travels from India to China and on into Japanese lore.

Some of the earliest illustrated were birds, whose beaks transmogrified into noses over the centuries. Nowadays Tengu is regarded as a slayer of vanity, and most certainly with a nose like that and a complexion that signals fury, any form of self-love would seem to be out of the question.

But then more than a few guys come into this world with an almost inbuilt sense of self-worth and entitlement, so maybe he does think and see himself as a pretty handsome guy.

The last time Julia took a look — she likes to reach up and touch the spirited trio — she noted with concern that Tengu's nose had taken yet another knock. Maybe that was because I had used it to hang wet washing? Oh dear.

Laundry to be ironed (and I do try to keep it to the minimum, though being summer now and with us wearing so much cotton and linen, there is more than at any other time of the year) is piled in a rattan basket on one of two chairs.

Two folding tables leaning against the wall get pulled out for writing workshops; a stack of stools get pulled out for the monthly discussion group, based on the writings and teachings of Eckhart Tolle, that is held around the table in the dining room.

The anti-mozzy screen that in summer replaces one of the two sliding doors in the *genkan* leans up against the same partition over the winter, say from mid-October through to early June.

About half this right-hand wall (there is yet another cupboard behind it, but it's never used or opened) is taken up with a contemporary-style white cupboard. Originally used in the kitchen in the teahouse in Kamakura, it is now relegated to storing cables, tapes, tools and equipment.

On the floor beside this cupboard is my sewing machine in its box, and a large roll of brown paper, for taking patterns from the clothes I love so much and wear to pieces.

When Sandra called by the other day, she was surprised to see the machine out on the dining table, obviously in use.

"I never knew you sewed," she said, eyebrows disappearing out of sight, up into her hair.

"Well yes, on occasion," I replied.

Having edited craft books through the 1970s, I can very much do a bit of everything — knitting, quilting, patchwork, embroidery, dyeing, potting, wallpaper-hanging . . . Jill-of-all-trades and mistress of none has always summed me up.

Also my mother began her career as a fashion illustrator and spent much of her life dressmaking or teaching others to sew. I guess this is where my interest in textiles comes from, though I have been loath to admit it until recently.

She was a perfectionist when it came to her craft, and would tear open seams I had stitched in childhood with a strict, "Start again!"

Needless to say I rebelled in my teens and did not sew again until I had children of my own, at which point I was delighted to find I was in fact quite proficient.

Thanks, Mum.

The banner is a case in point. It lies rolled up on the high shelf that runs around the three stable walls of the room. Along with two enormous antique Chinese panels of lacquer and shells left by Michael, some golfing equipment being stored by Jeff (an occasional guest from Canada when, as a pro golf caddy, he fails to make the cut), the large flat red silk cushion used in *rakugo* performances, and innumerable boxes containing god knows what, but mostly, I suspect, empty.

Time for a clear out, for sure.

The banner could go too, of course, but I suspect that it may hang around as long as US policies in Iraq continue to reverberate.

I spent seven hours the night before the second protest march in central Tokyo in 1991, machining onto an ancient double bed sheet the anti-invasion/intervention message that it bears: US-UK coalition for peace against the US-UK coalition for war.

At the first rally, I had fallen in with a couple of journalists known from the Foreign Correspondents' Club of Japan and several other American and British guys — and by the end — disgusted at the poor turnout and lack of interest and passion — we had formed an alliance: next time we would walk together again, and with a banner.

Guess who — being the only woman — got the job of running one up!

We marched with it four times in all, and I'm told it even starred on TV. Well, it is very large and bold — a fine piece of work, if I say so myself.

Months later I sprayed it in red paint, both to symbolize the amount of blood being spilled in the name of liberation and democracy, and to show my disgust at the political games being played out in the name of power and profit.

Now I stand back from direct protest, for one thing hips and knees no longer allowing it, but acknowledge its place in effecting change. Paul Watson, the founder of the anti-whaling organisation Sea Shepherd, claims intervention is the only way. That is why he risks lives (including his own) to put his ships between whaling vessels and pods of whales; to stop them being killed. I am not so brave these days (though I like to think I might be if pushed), but I do respectfully admire such a stance.

And so I climb down off my political high horse and count three bags hanging from hooks, none of which I use. One is stuffed with bits of fabric (to one day make into something useful even though I never do), another contains *furoshiki* (Japanese carrying cloths); the last, a pale green shopping bag, is virgin: from Mexico, with an image of the Madonna printed on the side.

Only one framed picture in here, also hung on a hook. A poster advertising the indie film documentary *Senso (War) Daughters* (*Senjo no Onnatachi* in Japanese), first released in 1989, and directed by Noriko Sekiguchi in collaboration with Welsh cinematographer Chris Owens.

It won prizes at short film festivals in Melbourne and Toronto. Then in 1991 it was awarded the New Rising Director's Award at a two-day cinematic event focusing on the obstacles women have to overcome, at the Enoshima Women's Centre, just up along the coast road from Zushi.

It was at this time that I first interviewed Noriko; we subsequently kept in touch for several years. I remember at our first meeting she was reeling with surprise to have won another prize, this time from the Catholic Japanese Cinema Club.

"It's got shots of condoms, talks quite explicitly about contraceptive methods, both modern and traditional," she said, expressing genuine astonishment.

As I wrote at the time, *Senso Daughters* looked at the largely forgotten war fought by the Japanese against the Australians and Americans on Melanesia's Papua New Guinea.

It focused more narrowly on the women who lived through that period — islanders with whom Noriko lived for five years to gain their trust, and so-called comfort women, forcibly shipped out to sexually service the Japanese army — home-grown girls for the officers, Korean girls for the enlisted men.

Noriko has made several more documentaries over the years, all focused on Japan's responsibility for war wounds unattended, and the problems of Pacific islanders.

Interesting — a poster promoting a film protesting the consequences of war, a banner designed to protest the consequences of war, and both in an ironing room.

Maybe every time I lift the iron to smooth out a shirt or pair of trousers, I am subconsciously trying to eradicate the wrinkles and blemishes of misunderstanding and intolerance that set men at each other's throats, for whatever reason.

It's a thought, anyway.

P.S. I forgot to mention the room off the room, the additional storage space to be found to the left of the window, stretching under the stairs: a *nando* within a nando. It's full of stuff, stuff that I have not looked at for years and most probably never will again — until moving day.

The last time we really had any kind of a sort out was when we discovered termites were eating away at our underpinnings. They had chomped the front step of the *genkan* too, which is why that piece of new replacement wood along the edge is a different colour to the rest.

For two days, three men crawled under the house, treating the woodwork and replacing those parts most resembling sawdust. Coming so soon after the invasion of the raccoons, we really did feel under attack. But of course, it was far from personal.

Except that Akii lost the sleeves of many coveted record albums from the 1970s (Led Zeppelin especially was left near naked), munched from floor level through the cardboard box in which they were stored and upwards, one by one.

Termites eat anything cellulose.

It might be worth remembering that.

THE LIVING ROOM
washitsu no ima

Step across the corridor, slide open the *fusuma* doors opposite, and step up again. This time into a traditional Japanese room (*nihonma* or *washitsu*) with a floor area of eight *tatami* mats, laid to fit within a wooden base, and each a standard Tokyo region measure of 0.88 metres wide by 1.76 metres long.

Yes, tatami are different sizes in different parts of Japan, and that is my lesson of the day. Originally devised for the comfort of nobility, they didn't come into common use until the end of the seventeenth century, before which if you were poor you lived on rock-hard mud floors, with the occasional woven mat thrown on top if you were lucky.

According to the rules of Japanese *fuu sui*, or in the West feng shui, appropriated from China along with Buddhism (via Korea) in the sixth century and again given its own unique cultural twist, mats are laid with a view to good fortune. They are not laid in a grid pattern, which is considered inauspicious, and there is never any point when four corners meet.

Originally made of rice straw, tatami (meaning 'folded' or 'piled') are now more likely to consist of compressed wood shavings or even — the very term suggestive of unnatural sacrilege — polystyrene foam. Over this practical base is stretched the woven matting (tatami *omote*), made traditionally from a reed called *igusa*. Most is imported from Korea and China these days, but occasionally you may still find it being grown in Japan.

Twenty years ago, traveling in Kanazawa (Ishikawa Prefecture), I saw a dark green reed-like grass in a field and asked Akii to ask the farmer what it was. (This was way before I could enquire for myself!) "Igusa," came the reply, and the kindly man broke off a stem for me to smell and roll in my fingers. No one was more surprised than my dear husband, who had never considered the origin of omote before.

Fresh-made and -laid tatami is a lovely pale green in colour, with the most marvellous smell, like fresh-cut hay drying in the sun. The mats on which we live here were not new when we moved in, but already the subdued warm colour of pale honey.

Now they are even more knocked about, mostly due to everyday furniture (for which such flooring is not designed) being moved around: two blue upholstered seats (from the recycle shop Kuru Kuru in Zushi), which when stood side by side, make us feel we are on an aeroplane or traveling by train; two folding floor-level seats (LOFT, in Shibuya) with backs that provide support sitting up or lying down and removable cream-coloured cotton covers; and a black *kotatsu* (place of purchase long forgotten).

In traditional homes and many restaurants this low table

(kotatsu) has a pit underneath so that you can sit with your legs dangling down inside in comfort. But our own stands flat on the matting, with a removable top that allows a quilt to be laid over the table in winter so that warm air from the heater built into the frame underneath keeps feet warm. Sit on a *zabuton*, pull the quilt up around your waist and, with a warm *hanten* (padded jacket) on the top half, cosy comfort is ensured.

Healthy too.

In Kamakura and Hayama the heating was minimal, and if the temperature dipped we would simply put on more clothes. We rarely got sick, not the coughs and colds variety, anyway.

So now to the walls, only one of which, when I really look and think about it, is solid. With my back to the corridor, and looking ahead through the *engawa* into the garden, this one substantial wall stands to the left, so dividing this room from Akii's own.

To the immediate left, two deep tatami-to-ceiling cupboards, called *oshiire*, with sliding fusuma doors. The one nearest is used for storage — videos, DVDs, the kotatsu quilt in summer. It is also the route Tora takes every evening — her not-so-secret entry into the bowels of the house. She's made a hell of a mess of everything, with paw prints, scuff marks, rips and tears, but will not be deterred.

Yes, we could clip her claws, but never in two thousand years. The Bible has a lot to answer for when it talks of God giving Man dominion over the birds of the air, the beasts of the field, etc. Seems as if Christianity has been abusing Nature in His name ever since.

The cupboard to the right houses the TV, video and music equipment, and several Muji (Mujirushi) storage units of CDs. (Meaning, No Brand, 'Muji' is now ironically an internationally renowned brand in itself.) We liked the idea of hiding stuff away when not in use, especially in a room designed to celebrate tradition rather than the electronics age. So up rode Roberto when

we first moved in, his handyman tools and skills at the ready, and built in shelving so that everything fits.

The other half of this partition wall, finished in textured sand like all the other mortared walls in the house, is taken up by the *tokonoma*, or art alcove. A vertical tree trunk, stripped of bark and polished, acts as both a supporting pillar and a dividing marker.

Square-cut wooden pillars (*hashira*) are basic to the construction of the house, and stand throughout, more often than not, but not always, in corners.

Most of the timber is cedar, but on rare occasion hinoki, or Japanese cypress (*Chamaecyparis obtuse*) is expensively introduced. This slow-growing and beautifully-scented hardwood is used for incense and in the construction of temples, shrines and similarly traditional buildings of importance.

At the base of the tokonoma is a low matted shelf rising some ten centimetres above the regular tatami flooring, on which stand four items: a ceramic dish in brown and green shaped like a leaf, containing two fallen branches from the Chilean Auracanian pine; a woven lacquered bamboo sword stand bearing a hexagonal shaped vase in white and blue, with dried flowers; and a long flat box, the top inlaid with a delicate design of bamboo in mother-of-pearl (oyster shell).

I found the leaf while scouring recycle shops in Akiya with Catherine in the late 1990s.

The monkey puzzle tree droppings I picked up in a park in San Martin, Buenos Aires in November 1999. (For the full story, read *Chasing Shooting Stars*, first published in 2013.)

Being a collector of military memorabilia, my Argentine-born Chilean cousin's son Pablo would love to get his hands on the sword stand, but not yet. Maybe I'll take it with me next time I go to visit, give him a surprise.

The vase, with Chinese lettering and a mountain view, came from a junk shop in Kobe (while visiting to interview the admirable writer Meira Chand in Rokko in 1987 — a story in itself but not one that I am keen to resurrect for either of our sakes. Best to let sleeping cats lie, so to speak).

Knowing my passion for bamboo — I had been photographing it for several years, and had also written about the Bamboo Museum in Beppu, on Kyushu island, with great enthusiasm — Akii gave me the box as a birthday present, another recycle shop treasure.

A scroll hangs on the wall behind. A typical Chinese scene of mountains, water and clouds, with Man painted to scale to resemble the insignificant ant he is, we are. As Akii says, he knows that, as an artwork, it's not very good, nor was it very expensive, but he bought it for me as an *omiyage* in Taiwan, on one of his own independent trips. So I am fond of it.

All of which makes me reconsider the painting in the corridor, and remember that it was purchased in Nanjing. Akii thinks his father may have been there during the war, and he wanted to see with his own eyes what Japanese history denies. After walking around the War Museum, dedicated to the 300,000 Chinese who died during the Nanjing Massacre, we went to see what its shop had to offer.

As if to alleviate our anger and shame, we left with the painting most likely to heal wounds: a gentle cloudscape with mountain tops and nary a human being in sight.

Okay, now I have my back to all just described, and look to my right, towards the open door where I entered.

To its left in the corner, a small *tansu* (storage chest) with shelves and drawers. I keep sewing stuff inside. On the main shelf, a black plastic box in traditional Japanese design containing matchboxes — freely given away here in bars and restaurants as 'service'. And for balance, a hand-thrown stoneware bowl containing ancient potpourri and run around the outside with partridges — another of Jill's lovely ceramics.

There is also a metal comb for helping Tora shed her heavy winter coat as the weather warms towards summer. She likes to sprawl on our laps as we all watch TV.

On the top of the tansu, with its dark wood and rounded corners, stands a lamp, rather the worse for wear but much treasured. I bought it at the Crafts Centre in Naha on Okinawa Island in 1992, and then carried it carefully back by air and train to Honshu and home. Made from bamboo and *washi* paper, the light itself is encircled and so shaded with a length of the hand-woven fabric known as *bashohfu*, created from banana plantain.

The famed *haiku* poet, Bashoh (Matsuo Munefusa, who walked seventeenth-century Japan, named himself after the fine stand of this plant growing outside his house. (His travels are described in *Oku no Hosomichi*, or *The Narrow Road to the Deep North*; his haiku or seventeen-syllable verses are famed and, three centuries later, widely known internationally.)

Today, travelling around Okinawa, it is still commonplace to see bashoh growing in gardens, for the simple reason that traditionally it was used for weaving. With a source of fibres for creating clothing, a well for fresh water, fishing on your doorstep, good soil for growing vegetables and rice, and a semi-tropical climate, it was not so difficult to be self-sufficient.

One good reason why Okinawan people have been so long-lived is that they live the good life. Or they did so until the US came along in 1945 and in the process of liberation and occupation, once again did their best and worst to turn a unique and ancient culture upside down and inside out.

An early rehearsal for Iraq, maybe.

We had stayed at the famed Daiichi Hotel in Naha where the owner, Shimabukuro-san, had some twenty lamps on display made by one particular artist. Later, when I spotted a new one for sale in the city's craft centre I snapped it up (before she did).

This lovely inn, with just eight guest rooms, was also where I first saw flower petals scattered on water on a plate — in that instance, a single red rose among a scattering of tiny pale pink petals above white pebbles — to signify welcome on the floor of the entrance way. Shimabukuro-san was sixty then; today she will be in her late seventies, a realisation that comes as a tremendous shock somehow, because (crass though it sounds) that trip — like so many others — seems like just yesterday. Time playing tricks again.

However, it appears that the hotel is still laying out its superlative breakfast — all those homemade preserves in antique cut glass bowls — so presumably this energetically stylish force for the good and beautiful is still going strong.

I do hope so.

I hope also that my children and their spouses are getting along famously. There are photos of them here — a black-and-white of Lee and Buffy taken by their junior school teacher, a kindly long-haired and bearded New Zealander who taught Lee how to play chess, roundabout 1970; no idea where Ray is now.

Alongside, a collage of cut-out-and-stick colour

snaps from the 1990s, showing son-in-law Ross in fine athletic form jumping off the steps of their new/old house in King Street, Toronto, and Buffy with her beloved white boxer Nellie (sadly, now deceased). Also the two of them together with Lee, but the girlfriend of that time covered over with Susan, whom he wed in 2007. (These things are tricky.)

A third photo leans against the wall, showing a young pregnant woman with swinging chin-length blonded hair (very 1960s) sitting on a chair, facing a small boy with blonde curls. They are looking into one another's eyes with great attention, and while she is obviously speaking to him, I have no memory of what it was I was saying to Lee. I know only that it was part of a photo shoot for a syndication company in London called Camera Press, for which

I was paid, but not enough to make a difference, and for all I know the negs and contact sheets are still in their files.

This picture of us has been important to me over the years, especially when relations became strained. I would look at it and remember — know in my bones — the depth of the loving connection between us.

The connection between all three of us, for Buffy is my second gracious gift, again born with infinite loving wisdom.

A rail runs around the room, the structure as always being essentially a frame with infills. Propped on top is a painting bought in Australia when visiting Louise and Fred that first time, soon after they married in Sydney.

I have known Louise since the mid-1970s, when we worked on a book together, so for over forty years. Another shock to the system — such a long time ago!

But back to the picture, painted by an Aboriginal artist from the northeast area of the continent . . . but now I come to take it down and look, I remember that the details are sealed inside the frame. At the time I thought it the only place to keep them safe; now hoisted by my own petard, I am rendered blind and ignorant by my own decision.

Well, suffice to say it's a very fine 'Dreaming' and I admire it greatly, being in earth tones and depicting women hunting for potato tubers; there is a double circle in the centre (their village, protected) and then tracks of footprints out into the bush, with half-circles to show where the women bend down with their baskets and digging implements. The edible roots are white squiggles of paint that look like worms, until you know better. I had it set off in silver on wood, which suits well enough, except I now see the frame as Made in Taiwan.

There is a small dancing Hindu goddess in hammered metal relief on the doorpost. Bought at a stall in Bangkok, I can still

remember picking her up and feeling a frisson of what I can only describe as pleasurable recognition. That was in 1994 and we were en route to Chiang Mai, a very different place to how it is now, I'm told on good authority.

Or was it on the way back?

Hmmm. My memory is terrible these days . . . another reason to get what I can recall down on paper as quickly as possible. What is clear in my mind is a picture of the street on which I bought her, and the worn but smiling face of the stall-keeper.

No, I did not haggle over the price. It sickens me that European tourists — especially the young ones who, while on gap-year budgets, are still infinitely more advantaged than the large majority of Thailand's local population — brag of beating down the natives to save a few baht.

What did she cost? No idea. I've forgotten. It's not important. Nor does it matter what she is worth, this being directly linked to my appreciation of her existence and the craftsmanship that brought her into being, which makes her priceless.

She dances, lightly pinned into place below a small box containing two ancient First Nation (indigenous Canadian) arrowheads, chipped and shaped from flint.

They were a gift from Lyle Thurston, who died not so long ago in Vancouver, prematurely really, as he was only seventy. But he had played as hard as he worked, making what friends often regarded as bad choices in terms of intimate relationships in later years, possibly linked to being knocked down by a bicycle in 1980, an accident from which many feel he never really recovered.

There is an old joke that if you go into a bar anywhere in the city of Vancouver you will end up sitting next to someone who claims to be a founder member of Greenpeace.

Well Lyle was exactly that, borne out by the fact that several hundred friends, supporters and admirers turned out to celebrate his life in memoriam on June 21, 2008, on the grassy area of Vancouver's Jericho Beach, between the concession stand and the yacht club.

Mutual friend Janice, who helped organize the event, reports that there was a lot of dancing that day too!

She recalls: "We had a picnic on what would have been his birthday. There was a photo gallery, with laptops set up. Also sound stages for music, and microphones for speeches. The singer, Al Neil, credited Lyle with saving his life (after an overdose). Former judge

Nancy Morris told some stories so uniquely Lyle that everyone was in hysterics . . ."

A doctor, well known in the community for running medical services at rock concerts and treating young drug addicts, Lyle was also a patron of the arts — he was especially fond of classical music and the ballet — and a lifetime environmental advocate.

In 1971 he closed his practice for two months to join eleven other activists on the fishing boat Phyllis Cormack, acting as the crew's medic as they sailed north to Alaska, to protest against nuclear testing in the Aleutian Islands.

That was the first Greenpeace campaign.

During its second campaign, to stop French nuclear testing in the South Pacific, Lyle helped set up the organization in London. He also carried the Greenpeace flag into the Vatican, the story being that when he slipped out of the official meeting for a cigarette (the drug of his choice), the Pope happened to come past and gave him a blessing.

Lyle gave generously of his time, expertise and commitment and in 1979 was a co-founder of Greenpeace, encouraging others to set aside the original legal structure and adopt a new international Board of Directors.

It was Nikolas who first introduced us. Lyle was staying with him in Tokyo's Yotsuya — old friends from the days when Nik danced with the Royal Ballet and Lyle was in love (and forever remained in love) with one of its principal prancers.

Nik remembers asking me to recommend an *onsen* (hot spring), which I did, but the visit was not successful; Lyle hated the experience. But he never held it against me, and was sweet enough to take me to lunch the first time I passed through Vancouver on my way to Buffy, in Toronto, to visit Nik, who had moved there in 1998.

After a morning in the Museum of Anthropology, I was feeling quite blown away: bowled over, both by its magnificent collection of totem poles, and the work of Emily Carr (1871–1945), who painted indigenous people and their culture along the Pacific North-West coast long before mainstream European immigrants showed any interest.

No doubt many of my comments and questions were disingenuous, but Lyle took them bravely on the chin. No doubt the wine helped! We spent the whole afternoon in a tiny bistro, and never have I been so enchantingly entertained and educated.

On a later trip with Akii, also on our way to Toronto, we stayed with Lyle in his divinely situated house on Vancouver's Deep Cove, overlooking the water.

By this time nothing could disguise the fact, however, that Lyle was letting things slide . . . there were dead mice on the kitchen floor and trails of blood, and I'm none too sure the bed sheets were clean.

However, the acoustic advantage of the open plan arrangement of floors and stairways made up for any slack: the memory of Anna Moffo's heavenly soprano voice echoing through the house, honouring Verdi as no other, is one that I will never forget.

For breakfast he took us to what he jokingly called The Lesbian Coven, a restaurant just along the waterfront run by women who served up the most heavenly pancakes imaginable.

Nik and Mark and others spent a lot of time with Lyle on Vancouver Island's West Coast in the last year of his life; he loved it there, especially Wickaninnish Island, in which he had a share. He had stayed with us in Hayama on at least one occasion, which being by the sea (but on the other side of the Pacific) helped make him feel at home.

Good times had by all.

A square silk bag made in Nepal now hangs off Lyle's box of arrowheads — they were very precious to him and I was touched that he would give them away, or rather maybe hand them on for caretaking?

Woven with an image of Buddha, the bag was gifted by my former yoga teacher in Hayama. Kei (whose Ashram Chetana is now in Zushi but sadly I no longer practice, knees disallowing) is as tiny and as fragile-looking as they come, but she climbs and treks mountains in Nepal with an energy and determination that confounds.

I don't know why I hung it over Lyle's box of arrowheads, but it looks right, feels right, and therefore in some mysterious inexplicable way must be right.

Which brings us neatly to the *kamidana* (literally 'god shelf'), across the other side of the doorway and situated — also quite rightly — up high. Every self-respecting Japanese house has one, just as most modern-built houses, however eclectic in architectural design — with bow windows, Doric columns, cottage gardens — have at least one tatami room in a tip of the hat to tradition.

Traditionally kamidana incorporate a Shinto shrine, honouring the animist belief that all things have spirit, are made up of divine energy. Dogma-driven religions regard Shinto as pagan, and indeed many festivals associated with its celebratory rites — marriage, birth, fertility — do touch on something primeval in the human psyche. Note that I do not use the word primitive, as this insults the essential truth and reverential depth of many ancient forms of worship.

There is a kamidana in Harada, our local family restaurant in Zushi, with cut white paper for purity, and offerings of fruit and sake rice wine to gratify the gods and keep them smiling. (To reduce confusion, sake is pronounced sa-kay.)

There are a dozen or more in Californian Colleen's home — part of a temple complex in Akiya — because she collects them, as artefacts.

My own treatment of kamidana also breaks a few rules, but whereas my husband's aunt Sumiko was profoundly shocked

when she first realised what I had done, hopefully the gods themselves are not offended, because they are altogether, in one place, signifying my own innate sense and belief that God is One and beyond comprehension, made personal (and dogmatic) only by national and cultural beliefs in the name of exclusion.

So here, happily rubbing shoulders with local gods and goddesses is Buddha, represented by a print of the blind Chinese priest Ganjin, who is credited with bringing Buddhism to Japan in the eighth century. It took him twelve years to make the journey after being first invited to act as a spiritual guide; he then stayed for another ten, living over half this time in the temple he founded in Nara in 795, Toshodai-ji.

In Sanskrit, the "shodai" of Toshodai reads as 'vast and wide', like the sea and land and cultural divide he crossed.

As if in celebration of this coming together, indigenous spirits and messengers from all over are one happy family — Australia (a bark painting, with boomerangs and dancing warrior spirits),

Canada (small painted totem pole found in a junk shop on Queen Street in Toronto . . . also a carved eagle purchased from Chris and Shirley's wonderful shop and gallery in Victoria (dedicated to providing work for First Nation craftspeople), two rough-hewn rice gods from the Philippines, and an African figure carved as smooth as ebony.

A slender Hindu god stands beside the figure of a peasant woman from the 1960s, carrying a sickle for cutting rice and a hat to guard against working in open fields, carved from soapstone. Being very heavy, in both physical weight and the burden of her Maoist place in history, her presence seems to upset the righteous more than any other.

Just another -ism, I explain: Judaism, Sufi-ism, Buddhism, Shintoism, Animism, Socialism, Druidism, Capitalism, Imperialism, Communism . . . each and every one a philosophical way of looking at the world and initially at least designed to try and make sense of it for the common good.

There is music too . . . a pair of cymbals from Bhutan (thanks, Rita), also a beaten metal bowl from Myanmar . . . not that I have ever been there, nor will go until the current regime changes, but it was a gift from a merry angel. (I used to hit the side for a lovely sweetly ringing chime when I lit incense; now it contains sand from the beach to hold incense sticks.)

Oh, and hiding away between the lot, a small angel cast in silver to contemporary design. I tried to take it to former writing student George Deutsch — he being a Jewish-Christian-Buddhist by studied evolution — when he was in the St Luke's hospice in Tokyo in May 2010, but when I returned home found it still in my pocket.

I like to think that when he died the following month he was strong enough to fly off on his own uplifted wings, without any help from me, or anyone else for that matter. Anyway, the mini-angel is now restored in place, gathering dust with all the other spiritual entities.

There were several years when my kamidana was incredibly important and supportive. But these days, less so, as grief over my mother's death in the summer of 2007, swiftly followed by that of my younger sister, Bridget, gives way to mourning and acceptance, and the centre fold of my being holds ever more solid and true.

During the last month, though, I have on several occasions lit incense and recited "AUM" three times to commemorate Akii's father's passing; I like the way the sound reverberates in three different ways throughout my whole body, leaving me calm, energized and present.

But I have not felt the need for several days now — for these rituals are for us, not for the deceased, who are long gone and busy working out what was learned and not learned in their previous timeline on Earth and so preparing for their next reincarnation.

This has nothing to do with belief, however; more to do with a knowledge lodged deep in my bones.

Azzah is preparing for her own spiritual rebirth in Mexico, where she is studying the teachings of the Russian mystic and seeker Gurdjieff. An accredited psychologist, she came here to Japan for many years to counsel and run workshops in personal growth and development and is, I suppose, now as much a dear friend as therapist.

We stayed with her in San Miguel de Allende, north of Mexico City, over the New Year in 2007. During which time Omar, her partner at that time, took Akii in his truck to source foodstuffs for the restaurant he worked for, so allowing him an inside view of Mexico that few are privilege to, while Azzah and I batted about in her battered VW Beetle, checking out hot springs, ancient ruins, crystal mountains and other spiritual hotspots.

It was she who, on her way to Narita from Kansai, brought us the lovely head of a *kannon* (Goddess of Mercy) that hangs beneath the kamidana.

Cast in iron from some ancient original, the mask is dated Showa 38, meaning 1963, so it is vintage if not antique. The Japanese characters also identify her to have been created to commemorate the founding seven hundred years before of Kokudan-ji temple in 1263. I can find no trace of a temple of this name in Kyoto, where Azzah said she bought the piece, but no matter: she's very lovely.

(Yes, Azzah, you too!)

The top of the mask is filled with dried hydrangea flowers from the garden, so they resemble a crown. Such is its peaceful grace — the calm of countenance divine — I am reminded very much of the Daibutsu (Big Buddha) in Hase, Kamakura, a favourite place of pilgrimage, especially in the early morning, by bike, ahead of the crowds.

Azzah: Jewish mother from Ukraine, Sufi father from Ossetia. Emigrated to Australian when she was six . . . a little Muslim girl with a shaved head, much bullied.

Ran away as a teenager to live with Aboriginal families in the Bush, where strong intuitive non-verbal communication skills were both understood and appreciated.

Taught herself to read and write in late teens, travelled the world studying with shamans, gurus and healers and surviving by becoming as street-wise as they come, even to the point of selling cow dung as garden fertilizer.

Worth a book in her own right, for sure . . . or at the very least, a long strong chapter.

Now, stand in the corner where kamidana meets fusuma and look diagonally across the room, to where hangs an androgynous-looking but maybe male Hindu angel from Bali, made from jointed wood pieces (his wings come off) and painted and gilded.

There is no memory of how he came to be in my life . . . I guess he just flew in one day, decided we needed his help (or liked the look of us) and chose to stay.

To his left are four doors of thin old glass covered with *shohji* — latticework panels of wood papered with washi that slide up and down to allow light to enter the room from the *engawa* and garden beyond.

We keep them raised most of the time, but only because otherwise Tora tends to have a field day, ripping the paper to bits. She thinks it a lot of fun, but Akii is the one who does the repapering! By choice, I hasten to add; he says he finds the stripping, cutting and pasting therapeutic.

The wall to the right of our colourful angelic protector is made up of four solid wooden panels, the two centre ones sliding back over the others for a view of and entry into the dining room.

Above the rail are several fans used in summer, and a framed philosophical chastity belt. Which is how the small embroidered

purse on strings was described to me on my first trip to Hokkaido in the late 1980s, and the hot spring resort of Noboribetsu.

I found it in an antique shop, where a fine-looking man with bushy eyebrows and piercing but kindly eyes explained as best he could to a foreigner with no more than a few words of Japanese, that it had been embroidered by an Ainu woman with the name Mariko Mikami, who had died in 1986 (the year I arrived in Japan) aged just fifty.

The *katakana* characters for mi-ka-mi ma-ri-ko are written on the back. (Katakana is the alphabet devised to spell out all non-Japanese words, so indicating that native Ainu were not considered to be Japanese.)

It seems that Mikami-san was well known for making a study of Ainu clothing and embroidery when few were interested; there is even a book. I had recognized the symbols, worked in chain stitch, to be Ainu, but assumed it to belong to a child.

Well, yes and no, it was intimated (assuming I was correctly understanding what he was trying to say): it was made for a young girl to symbolize her virginity.

Beyond that he, as an Ainu man, could not say.

Much has been written about the plight of the Ainu people, also known as Ezo, who were first pushed northwards off Honshu, the main island of Japan, by the Japanese, and then — in what the government decreed to be a process of assimilation — persecuted and encouraged into inter-marriage to near extinction.

It was not until very recently — June 6, 2008, to be exact — that Japan granted them official recognition as an Indigenous People. Better late than never, some might say. For a whole way of life, however, it is too late.

Having said that, a significant number of people with Ainu blood are trying to preserve and resurrect what remains of tradition and culture, as exemplified in the summer of 2009, at a festival in the seaside park in Kanazawa-bunko, between Zushi and Yokohama.

Here Ruben, staying locally with friends James and Reiko, sat down with Ainu elders and, as Water Messenger of the Hopi tribe in Arizona, exchanged greetings and offered prayers.

Nearby, a stall offered T-shirts and books, and samples of musical instruments based on surviving originals.

The best place to see such artefacts? The Batchelor Memorial Museum, in Sapporo's Botanical Gardens, which was dusty and deserted when I visited twenty-plus years ago. There is another fine museum now near Noboribetsu, but steer clear of so-called Ainu villages, which are nothing more than tourist traps.

No, it was in John Batchelor's house — he was a minister in the Meiji period (1868-1912) who felt as passionately about Ainu culture in general as Mikami-san did about the specifics of decorative symbolism — that I first saw and fell in love with embroidered clothing that stopped me in my tracks, and salmon skin accessories that defied all logic: imagine, fish boots!

Which brings me down to ground level again, and the few remaining items in this room worthy of note.

Three *zabuton*, covered in *kasuri*, courtesy of Catherine.

Four soft cushions scatter a couple of floor-level seats: two appliquéd with black cotton geometrics on a dark purplish-blue ground; one in white cotton embroidered with lines of running stitch in pale blue thread in the style known here as *sashiko*; the last in cotton yarn, and knitted in moss stitch with five wooden buttons for closing.

(Yup, made this one myself!)

There are also two more lamps: one in the corner under the kamidana, the other on the far side of the tokonoma. Both are pierced, to allow light to flow, but here all similarity ends.

One is a length of lacquered bamboo punched with innumerable holes to resemble a lotus flower, stood upright on a wooden plinth on top of one of the music speakers. Artist Maki made it, and I can only say her patience and tenacity are much to be admired.

The other light is much larger and ceramic, this time courtesy of Yuko, who also lives in Yamanone and has a studio, on the way to Alex and family in the next valley.

A full-time potter, Yuko was much influenced by Mesopotamian culture when we first met, and so we have a floor-standing zigzag-style ziggurat, slipped geometrically in triangles of lovely earthy tones — brown, ochre, orange — with diagonally placed slit windows from top to bottom.

Akii complains that the room is dark in the evenings, even with three lamps lit.

But that is because he grew up with neon.

'nuff said.

THE SUN ROOM
engawa

Japanese people use the *engawa* as a halfway-house between domestic life inside and the natural world without.

Heather, who was born in Ontario, Canada but has lived down the Shonan coast near Enoshima for over three decades and is possibly the most successfully encultured non-Japanese I've met to date, explained recently in a writing exercise how she uses it to move between two cultures:

The engawa is the space between a tatami room and the outside. Open the sliding glass doors, close the shohji walls, and you are on a bench outside. Close the glass doors and open the shohji onto the tatami, and you are indoors. It is a great space to relax in, reading or visiting. It is also a great space in my life. I can close and open certain windows and doors and let myself be in Japan, or in a Western world. Maybe that is why I love the ambiguity of Japan. It lets me alternate between living like a local, or like a foreigner. This applies to almost all aspects of my life: social, culinary, household, entertainment. It is my safety valve, my cushion, which lets me slip in and out of these two worlds.

So let me step from my own world of interior into that of the in-between, signified by the parting of the *noren* (a divided curtain) to allow me through.

I bought this in an antique market at Morito-jinja between Zushi and Hayama when Catherine and Graham were here. Also Canadian, but from British Columbia, their house in Akiya was pivotal to a whole circle of multicultural social activity on this part of the Shonan coast back in the late 1990s.

Anyway, Catherine and I pounced on this tangle of curtains, which are hung on poles outside pubs and restaurants, bathhouses and even some stores to announce they are open for business. We each picked one out, delighting in the fact they were loosely woven from flax and dyed with indigo. Definitely for summer rather than any other season, we agreed.

My noren is much faded now, and falling to pieces, but still, I cannot quite bring myself to replace it. Catherine's own? No idea.

Mr and Mrs Perfect's marriage fell to pieces big-time after six months back in Victoria. Now Graham is with Bo in Northern Thailand, in the house G(raham) & B(o) built. And after some difficult years, Catherine has reconnected with innate physical and internal strengths to reframe her life with a different set of priorities.

She now bats backwards and forwards between Victoria and Laos, where she works with Rassanikon, founder of the Nikone Handcrafts

Centre in Vientiane, and who has selflessly devoted her life to promoting traditional weaving and establishing markets abroad.

Last heard of, Catherine was packing to carry a vast métrage of commissioned hand-woven silk back to George — curtains for his house in Florida. She is now teaching in Vientiane, which is great news.

The wooden-frame chair in which I sit to read in sunlight through the seasons came from that period when she and Graham were together. When they packed up to return to Canada after a decade in Japan, it was one of a pair that they decided to leave behind.

We have one; her brother Alex, who lives over the hill in the valley adjacent to our own here, the other. Sometimes when reading in this chair, with its 1920s Art and Craft movement design and loose cushioned seat and backrest, I will it to Alex (now married to Rikako and with daughter Nina) in the full knowledge that while we may (near impossible though it be to imagine) move on at some point, they will always be here.

But it may be best not to be so definite. After all, as life demonstrates from day to day, second to second, however well you think you know people and what is happening in their lives, you never know what is really going on or going to happen, and most probably a good job too.

A small over-stuffed tapestry cushion has cornered the chair, but loses out when I sit down, more often than not ending up on the rug. My mother stitched it . . . one of the very last pieces she completed before her hands became unsteady and she could no longer hold the needle. I love the traditional Celtic design in varying shades of green on creamy beige, a pattern that, in its complex spiralling, has no visible beginning and no known end. As with her soul journey . . . as with my own . . .

Mum's Cushion (as I call it) looks at home wherever it hangs out, even on the rug, which is odd because the cultural heritages of these two pieces of furnishing are so extreme — one from so far west as to

be almost in the Atlantic, and the other so far in the east that it lies between the Euphrates and the Tigris, on the very edge of Asia.

Byron, from whom I bought the rug for three hundred dollars when we first moved in here, was sure of its provenance — from Iraq, tribal, a rug woven from sheep wool and camel hair, on which a family would sit and eat. What first called to me, though, was the minimalist modernity of the pattern, which is so simple that it might have been designed today. It was then I learned of its history. Byron does not specialize in Middle Eastern floor coverings, but

rather religious artefacts from Japan and roundabout. His house in Tokyo's Shinanomachi — an astonishing antique hangover from the past in itself, dating from the Edo period (1603-1868) — brims over with gods and goddesses, Buddhist statuary, animist effigies and carvings galore. Spooky to sleep in, some might think. But having made them his business as well as his family, Byron has no trouble at all.

He has built up a loyal clientele over the years, with buyers all over the world. Busier than ever, I hear, especially via eBay.

Behind me, against the solid partition wall, stands Glen and Michael's *tansu* — the one they left behind in 2006 on their return to England. Yes, they did call by this summer while visiting, but no, despite acknowledging once again how very beautiful it is, they have a brand new apartment and all mod cons, where it really wouldn't fit. So I guess here it stays, for the time being at least.

On the top shelf, two baskets — one so finely woven it must have cost Sandy an arm and a leg, and the other another maverick *gomi* find.

Also the largest seed pod imaginable, imported from the jungles of Southeast Asia by Gaku and Mariko; they run the small organic bakery-cafe in Hayama called Khanompan, and often cook Thai dishes for lunch. I use it as a starting point in writing classes sometimes. I lay it on the floor where to me at least it looks like a rearing snake and ask, "What is this? Half close your eyes, what does it resemble? Where is it from? What does it say to you? Where does it take you?"

On another shelf, a wooden shoe last from Mexico, painted with cacti and a donkey — a gift from Omar, one of whose family members was a shoemaker. I wonder where he is, what he is doing, now that he and Azzah are no longer an item? The more I write, the more I realise how much of the stuff and fabric of my life is connected to the parted and the departed.

Which makes me think . . .

There's nothing much more here. A white lamp from Muji that stores energy and can be lifted up and carried around during the power cuts that tremors sometimes instigate; such a clever design

company! Two metal stands (very hip in their day) for CDs dating from when Nik left. A large bronze antique container — a *hibachi* once used for heating charcoal in winter but now housing a ginger plant run rampant.

Also floor-standing, and designed to house smoking coils of incense (*senko*) to deter mosquitos, a small dark lidded ceramic tower that is showing cracks, from the time Rika accidentally banged it with the floor cleaner and it shattered into pieces; I came back from town to find her and her small daughter Mone sitting on the floor, tearfully trying to glue them back together, perhaps in the vain hope I might not notice.

No, nothing of genuine value, though now that I look carefully, I see how the number three runs like a repeating chorus through the space: rows of three times three for nine circular motifs, white on brown, patterning the flat chair cushion pads; three sprigs of what is most commonly known as the 'wealth' plant, a succulent that is reputed to attract or create abundance.

My money's on either *Crassula ovata,* also known as Jade Plant or Friendship tree; or *Pilea peperomioides* — the Chinese Money Plant, Lefse Plant, or Missionary Plant, from the south of China.

Whatever, whichever its heritage, stands on the left-hand arm of the chair, in a terracotta pot, soaking up the sun and creating plenty for all.

The mosquito ceramic stands on the rug on three feet that curl upwards; the knob on top is a three-way twist. In between, slots to allow the smoke to escape echo the design of the lamp that Yuko also made. As for the hibachi, the handles are three-petalled fleur de lis, with metal rings.

How interesting that I have never made this connection before, and I so so-called observant. Ha! We really do go through life deaf, dumb and blind, set on automatic pilot, even on those rare occasions we like to think of ourselves as even remotely present;

if we are thinking, of course, we are in our minds, not the moment.

And herein lies the error of our ways . . . with sixty to eighty thousand monkey-mind thoughts flying through our minds every single day — too much bloody thinking.

I lean back from my book and look up into the ceiling, painted white with wooden laths nailed into place. There are watermarks, stains, signs of leakage. This too is new to me.

I realise that like the noren, the house is disintegrating around me . . .

That time and money need to be spent . . .

That love has made me blind.

THE DINING ROOM

yohshitsu no dainingu ruumu

There can surely be no less aesthetic sight than a ceiling covered with polystyrene tiles.

Few rooms get away with it, but for some reason, the dining room downstairs (and my study upstairs) cope rather well. Though it could be that I have simply learned to do what the Japanese do — edit out the negative and focus on the positive.

If the house was our own, of course, they would have come down long ago, but it's not, so I live in forbearance. The lights, however, had to go — two large squares of neon, secreted behind sheets of washi paper; the light so much softer now, with few noticing how the effect has been achieved.

The positive aspects of the space we so grandly call the dining room are all to do with wood — a gleaming parquet floor and all the walls (vertical posts and horizontal timbers in-between) panelled. You can walk into it same-level from the corridor, kitchen, guest room and bathroom, but have to step down from the tatami room.

Sometimes visitors forget and go flying . . . and not only visitors! There is a bruiser of a story here, but for the moment to be left hanging.

Centre stage stands a heavy, much bashed about oak table, with curving legs and carved decoration, and four solid wood chairs in simple shaker style.

We bought them when Leesa and Don moved on from Japan to La Madelena, a small piece of rock near Corsica in the Mediterranean that is home to one of the many US bases ringing the world.

Being naturally curious about Japan, Don (with Polish ancestry) a teacher on the Yokosuka Naval Base, the other side of the Miura Peninsula from Zushi, and Leesa, a home-grown slice of American apple pie with Italian roots, had decided to live off-base.

The large majority of so-called military families choose not to step outside the gates, but Don and Leesa were adamant that they did not fall into this classification, that they were independent.

Good for them, we — the gang, as we were back then — collectively agreed, and scooped them up.

Leesa especially changed a lot in her time here. A quilter, she became fascinated by Japanese weaving and dyeing techniques, began collecting her own dyestuff materials from the hills roundabout, and was soon designing quilted pieces that were more art than practical.

As she began winning contests and became quite famous, so her confidence grew and her technical prowess improved. It was wonderful to witness and I loved visiting her studio, seeing what she was up to.

A small framed collage that she gave me hangs at the entrance

to the kitchen — strips of greens in various vegetal hues laid to resemble a bamboo forest.

We were sad when they had to leave, but happy to take over their table and chairs. I think we handed over twenty thousand yen, which is ridiculous when you consider the wear we have got out of them. But then the table — which belonged originally to Leesa's grandmother — is American-Victorian (whatever that means — end of the nineteenth century, I suppose), so has been around the block a few times already.

What a story it will have to tell when it moves on again. Mind you, it needs a bit of repair, and at some point the central extending panel was removed, making it a table for six to eight rather than ten to twelve.

We gather around it to play Scrabble — a fun evening for Japanese students and friends learning English.

A different group — Swiss, Portuguese, German, Japanese, American, Canadian, English and Welsh — sits around it to discuss personal growth and spiritual development on the last Wednesday of the month. Initially we read the work of Eckhart Tolle; I then moved on to Leonard Jacobson's writings, workshops and retreats.

Writing students use the table to hone internal proprioceptive listening techniques for what we call "writes" (akin to soul searching on paper) after which we sit back and have lunch.

For parties I push it against the wall and spread a white damask tablecloth — one gifted by my aunt from Forneth House — to set off the buffet.

At the annual *rakugo* storytelling event in May, the audience perambulates around the table for snacks and soft drinks during the interval, and later, performers tuck into sushi and beer at the party afterwards.

Just recently, it now being January 2011, we put three assorted tables together and had twelve for Christmas dinner.

Generally, though, it is the place around which visitors congregate. Last evening, for example, Sonia came in with Julia, returning some books and borrowing a couple of DVDs. While Akii played noisy games with Julia (couple of kids, the two of them) Sonia and I caught up . . .

Soon after moving in here in December 2002, we had organised a house-warming party. Being an uncommon event in Japan, it created a bit of a stir, especially among our immediate neighbours, several of whom turned up on the day, unsure of the form, but open to the experience.

Among them was a couple in their early thirties carrying a

very new baby. Sonia proved to have been brought from her native Portugal to central Japan at age fourteen when her mother remarried a Japanese businessman.

It was in Nagoya, Aichi Prefecture that Sonia met Yuta, both of them working as DJs on a local radio station. They married, moved to Tokyo and then when Sonia became pregnant, to Zushi, which they believed was a healthier environment in which to bring up a child.

Now Yuta — Ito-*sensei* — has a holistic chiropractic practice in the town, and Sonia works as a freelance translator and interpreter, disappearing off at regular intervals to F1 motor and motorcycle circuits, TV stations and what the Japanese call *iro-iro*, this and that.

Being close, in every sense, they are a large, integral part of our life here, and Julia — now eight — regards us, I believe, as a second home. We are not her grandparents (she has two sets already) but more like buddies.

In fact, I remember walking with her in town one day and being stopped politely by someone who enquired of Julia if I was her granny or an aunt.

"Neither," said Julia, "Angela is my big friend."

I like that.

But back to the table and Don and Leesa, now transferred to Napoli, where she is reconnecting with her Italian roots big time.

We have not re-met since they left, but stay close enough, even to the point of encouraging them to use our cottage in Perthshire as a base for exploring Scotland. They stayed there in 2008, caring for the place like no other.

I mean, who do you know who would on holiday bother to use a toothbrush to clean the sliding mechanism of the doors of the shower?

Thanks, guys.

Jo, my aunt, would like them to come back too . . . apparently they were whizzes at weeding her beloved herbaceous border, and called by near on every day to ensure she was okay. She thought them a most excellent couple, and so do we, toasting them at this remarkably tolerant and welcoming heirloom table every day, whether in G&T, wine, sake, beer, coffee or good old English breakfast tea.

One point — in addition to the Mexican tray on the table, beaten from some light alloy that holds three ceramic whistles painted with images of the sacred temples of the Sun and Moon in Teotihuacan (reputed to be Aztec but with current excavations signifying far older cultures) and a pitch whistle for modern instruments, there are always fresh flowers.

Last week there were lilies; this week a vase of heavenly scented ginger flowers, some sprays of a purple flower unknown to me, and a bunch of mint, gifted by a student at last Saturday morning's class in Kotsubo.

I talk with this group in English only once or twice a month so it's no great burden; in fact it can be a lot of fun, especially since a recent class coincided with Halloween, so I had them apple bobbing, divining with apple peel, and dropping forks on yet more apples from a great height.

So yes, the main point: I would rather go without a meal than not have fresh flowers on the table.

Not sure what my children thought of this odd trait in their mother, when they were forced to eat baked beans on toast for breakfast, lunch or tea to ensure there were daffodils on the table in spring, roses in summer and home-forced hyacinths to bring colour and perfume to those dull days after the year-end. Remind me to ask them some day.

The general effect is that there is not much else in the room, but there is. To the left of the sliding door through to the *tatami* room, a hanger for displaying this and that from Tokyu Hands, into the transparent plastic pockets of which get tucked postcards (a Persian miniature, French maze, two feminist statements), also a birthday card from Buffy with that most inspirational quote by William Blake — you know the one: *"to see the world in a grain of sand, and a heaven in a wild flower, hold infinity in the palm of your hand and eternity in an hour."*

Plus memos, e.g., pick up anti-flea medicine for Tora Jeffs, as local vet Flipper addresses our dearly beloved cat. Photos: Buffy and Max (yes, I have a grandson now) in Toronto, Lee and Sue on holiday in Crete, Hiroko and Garth in Brisbane, Akii aged seven in Japan, and me ditto in England.

Akii already looks like a child needing to please the world; my own eyes resemble those of an abandoned puppy . . . or, even more bizarrely, an old-fashioned rocking horse, which is how Erich Fried — of whom much more much later — once described me.

In the pocket containing my photo is a cast off snakeskin, as found in the garden last year. I am a snake according to the old Chinese calendar, and to me life and death is surely nothing more than a series of casting offs of old skins to slide into yet another phase of energetic reincarnation.

The rest? A motley collection of memorabilia that comes by mail or hand, including, I note, a postcard from Sarah and Adrian showing *Le Labyrinthe (XIIe siecle)* on the floor of the Cathedrale de Chartres, from one of their once numerous trips to France to buy wine.

It must be quite old, this one, because now they divide their time between London's Queen's Park, an orange grove in Spain, and a rough and tumble apartment in a Roma village just down the road. The perfect life, I would say.

Not completely perfect, as no life ever can be with, as in their case, beloved grandchildren removed to Canada due to a messy divorce, but not half bad.

To the right, for a birthday from Catherine back in Victoria and framed, three tiny scraps of *kasuri* with some *sashiko* stitching (such immaculate taste, so clever with her hands). While above hangs a horse's head.

Okay, I know it sounds a bit odd, but it works, honestly. This equine beast is a long way from home also, having travelled here from a car boot sale just outside Oxford. I was there with Viv and Di and Mame, three roommates and dear friends from college (Bretton Hall, which was attached to Leeds University), who I was describing to Kathryn in an e-mail just this morning.

I had told her I was about to fly back for Viv's seventieth birthday party in November 2010 and Kathryn, a writer living in Shimokitazawa, Tokyo, noted that the idea of me jet-setting back to have fun with someone called Viv in Oxford, England, sounded incredibly exotic to her Indiana-born American ears. Not really, I replied:

She is Vivian, of course, the elegant (rather than exotic) one amongst the five of us — all drama students — who got thrown together for our first year in college in 1959. She married her dashing naval officer in a fairy tale wedding (with me in pink satin, selected because being so incredibly thin I was the best clothes hangar, amazing though it may seem now! Now Viv is handsome and stately and David is portly and looks a bit like Winston Churchill. Immensely kind, though . . . I guess there is a point at which we all settle for such attributes? Diana will be there, her knees as fine as ever, and looking every inch a Lady. Hilary died of cancer fifteen years ago in Australia; she married into showbiz and it took its toll. Mavis (Mame) died two years ago, also of cancer. Interestingly, these two lovely, feisty girls (as we all were) grew up just streets from one another in Todmorden, once a thriving textile mill town in Lancashire, and I always wondered if it was the environment that ultimately did them in. We have six daughters and five sons between us. Also, as far as I know, eight grandchildren . . . Funny, we were all going to be famous actresses. What happened?

So there were the four of us, the last time we were to be all together, rushing around this car boot sale in a field just outside Abingdon, with Di buying antique silver teaspoons (as she would), Viv picking up books and games for the grandchildren (ditto) and Mame . . . funny that, I can't remember exactly, but maybe books and games for her boys.

Anyway, I saw this horse's head and had to bargain hard, because it was clear the owner was ambivalent, not really wanting to see it go.

It was heavy and solid and kind of a daft thing to buy. But when I got back to London, Barry, who in parallel with film directing is a historian with a predilection for English oak, reckoned it to be medieval and quite possibly French.

So now Historic Object hangs in our dining room, half a world away, looking one hundred per cent distinguished in profile and equally comical face-on, with eyes asquint as if not quite sure what to make of the world. And who can blame him/her?

There is only one curtain at the window, and that hangs rather than ever being drawn. Pride of place goes instead to House Sprite with Tits and Thongs, as designed and made by Clara, who lives alone in an old house in Yokosuka, walks and cycles everywhere, thrives on next to nothing, and has a creatively strong inner life second to none.

Originally from Montreal, she has made and kept a diary for every year of her life since she was a small child . . . there are stacks of them filled with detailed accounts of this and that, quotations, illustrations, scraps . . .

She also makes dolls. But not your regular pretty dolls . . . rather figures from eccentric dreams and on occasion, it seems to me, the most ghastly nightmares.

House Sprite is made in some kind of knit fabric, kitted out from waist down in a sparkly skirt and, with a single string of pearls around her neck to offset her naked upper body, and hangs out twenty-four hours a day on a swing. Her tits are perky, her hands and feet wide and splayed and her face reminds me of a rat, crowned with a Mohican tuft of hair.

Not of this earth, for sure. Rather, a guardian spirit without equal.

On the floor below is a trunk with a flat kasuri-covered cushion on top stuffed with the husks of buckwheat *(sobagara)*. Beside this a fern-like plant with a life of its own . . . every time I talk to it I swear the fronds grow an inch.

The cabin trunk, though — empty, not really used very much, even as a seat — really ought to go, but as a historic marker it has to stay.

After my trip to Argentina, Chile and Uruguay in 1999, I began to write a book based on tapes made and adventures survived. Recovering from yet another breakdown, I began the slow crawl back to myself.

But my writing had slowed and come to a virtual stop until one day — living in Hayama as we were back then — I went to put out the *sodai gomi* for rubbish collection and there, cast away, was this enormous green leather-bound cabin trunk . . . you know, the kind rich people used to carry their copious belongings on transatlantic sea crossings; think the Titanic!

Opening up the lid, I was astonished to read that it had been made in Buenos Aires. Needless to say, I got the hint, dragged it back to the house, returned to my computer. My story, my book — *Chasing Shooting Stars* — was calling me back to get on with it. But let me draw a curtain on this part of my life, and get on with the next, assisted by that rough woven piece of hanging fabric in vertical stripes of red and white from Thailand, with no apparent practical use. It's a beauty, and holds the eye before leading one around the corner, from window to wall.

Here there are only a few pieces of what might be described as furniture, objets d'art or bric-a-brac.

The nice Japanese-style arts and crafts movement pegged bookcase by the window, courtesy of Glen when he left. I think I gave him five thousand yen for it. On the top, a square *washi* papered lamp (another recycle shop find); a brilliantly if eccentrically designed Italian kaleidoscope bought in an *onsen* hot spring in Himeji, famed for its castle; and a lighthouse.

Yes, that's right, a lighthouse: made to scale and painted white with a wide central band in crimson, light as a feather and yet crafted to last.

Turn it upside down and here, in a clear left hand, is scribed all you need to know: it's a model of the Kish Bank Lighthouse in the Republic of Ireland, as created by Brendan Patrick Eoin Conway, who had been a temporary lighthouse keeper in the 1980s.

Brendan had been stationed on Tuskar Rock, Skellig Michael, Fastnet Rock, Bull Rock, Rockabilly and Baily — such great names! He grew up on Wicklow Head, and holidayed at Mizen Head lighthouse when his father was stationed there.

Because his father had been a lighthouse keeper, and because of his own experiences, Brendan had always wanted to write a memoir . . . But he was blocked. Where and how to start?

By the end of his first workshop here in 2008 he had drafted two pages and subsequently kept going. However, he was experiencing difficulties in his personal life, eventually accepted a job in Australia, and tried to move on.

Before he left, though, he was immensely gratified to see a piece of his writing published in a specialist magazine.

Yes, there are magazines about lighthouses just as there are about boats and trains and planes.

A ray of light, you might say.

The wall that extends to the doorway into the guest room and bathroom, and beyond, is hung with pictures, each of which has a tale to regale. The latest to join the motley collection displays three ceramic *gingko* leaves — two larger and one small — mounted on a black plaque, with four labels on the back.

TO A LONG AND HAPPY LIFE 1, reads the first, being the first in a limited edition. Then there are two explanations of the subject, one in Japanese, the other in English: *The Gingko Tree is a living fossil, unchanged since the days of the dinosaurs, 250 million years ago. The symmetric fan-shaped "bilboa" leaf is a symbol of love, unity and longevity. "Bilboa" means two-lobed and symbolises the unity of two opposites: day/night, laugh/cry, male/female.*

There is more for those who would like to know: while native to China, the gingko (*gingko biloba*) in Japan is often to be found in the grounds of Buddhist temples and Shinto shrines, and since many are centuries old, they have sacred status.

When a thousand-year-old specimen in front of the third most important Shintoh shrine in all Japan, Hachiman-gu in Kamakura, blew down in a wind in 2009, the event caused such consternation that it made national news. Such momentous events tend to be regarded as bad omens.

Spiritual elements apart, the trees are loved for their golden leaves in autumn, and also the edible nuts which are eagerly collected in parks and streets as they fall and are a feature of traditional cuisine. Perhaps its most interesting characteristic is that this unique species has no close living relatives. A genuine one-off.

Finally, there is the name card of the Swiss-born artist and potter who created the piece, who came to Japan by way of America.

Putting all her energy into an appreciation of Japanese culture, Swanica developed a glaze that mimics the colour and refinement of Kamakura-*bori*, a form of lacquered woodcarving unique to the city where she finds inspiration, understanding and respect.

It did not bother me one scrap that the stem of one of the leaves on the artefact I bought had snapped off at some point. Swanica had glued it back together, but leaving a tiny crack of space between stem and leaf, so as to leave the observer in no doubt as to its accident-prone provenance.

This is something I have learned here: imperfection has its own reward.

With a younger sister who was severely challenged — Bridget both endured and embraced rheumatoid arthritis from age sixteen to when she died in 2007, just two months after our mother — I wish I had been more supportive and compassionate, but for many years (in fear and guilt) chose rather to turn away.

It took Japan to teach me, to bring the lesson home. She was amazing; I missed out on so much.

Below, slightly to the right, is a square-framed Navaho sand painting that Sonia and Yuta bought us as a Christmas present on a trip to Tokyo Disneyland. Considering that in less sensitive hands we might have ended up with pairs of Mickey and Minnie Mouse ears, we feel doubly blessed. Rather they browsed through some of the small stores around the theme park in Urayasu that specialize in ethnic crafts and goods from all over the world, and happened upon this.

Sonia says they chose it for the natural materials and colours, and also for its free-wheeling nature, with geometric faces at the end of four windmill-like arms, and feathered shadows in between to emphasise perpetual movement.

Interesting: on this same day of writing, I read that on October 19, 2010, the Hubble Telescope captured an image of a spiral galaxy (NG C 3982), describing it as: *a rich tapestry of star birth, along with its winding arms.*

Wanting to know more, I turned to a dictionary of American Indian symbols to learn that the image of whirling logs — representing the cyclic motion of life, seasons and the four winds — is frequently used in sand paintings by the Navaho; they consider it powerful medicine.

Some may see them as compass points; we like to think they keep us on the move, always changing, forever fired up, grinding the mill . . . The flaming heart of Jesus alongside, a "milagro" bearing a crown of thorns and beaten out of tin and painted, returned with us from Mexico. It is a common if ambiguous image in that part of the world, representing the passion of Christ and so blending faith in — and straddling the fence between — the Catholic church and ancient native religion and superstition.

Milagro means "miracle" in Spanish, and I have very personal reasons for choosing this image in a local market in San Miguel de Allende. As with all milagro, any associated image may indicate a body part — a broken heart to be mended, or a case of cardiac failure to be healed.

It came into my life too late to help my father, whose heart gave up the ghost in 1962.

But it was there, hanging around in the ether or my subconscious a decade later when my son came through major heart surgery; he was ten at the time. It had more substance in doing a great job when Lee had to go through more (but less crudely invasive) surgery in the mid-1990s to stop his heart short-circuiting.

Last year it was Richard's turn: Richard, back in London, who, having been in our lives for over forty years, suddenly became ill and needed heart surgery. And then had to go through the whole procedure a second time several months later.

He's had a hell of a year.

But he is still with us and he and Mimi (who had to supervise a house move, and then lost her mother in Chile amidst this nightmare) are slowly getting their lives back.

So whenever I pass my Mexican milagro, I touch it and say thank you, not because I am religious, but because it does no harm and may do good in ways we cannot hope to understand, ever. After all, isn't that what faith is all about?

There are two photos of my children, higher up and further along.

In the first, Lee aged around four is sitting on grass in the back garden of Mondesfield, the house in Exeter Road in London's Kilburn where we lived in a first floor rented flat for the first ten years of his life.

He is holding ten-month-old Buffy on his lap, his face expressing a loving gravity that speaks volumes about his sense of responsibility and loyalty, even at so early an age.

The second is a triptych — three photos, also in colour, but technically much improved since 1966 — mounted one above the other rather than horizontally.

Buffy is topmost, wearing her straw hat and sunglasses; Lee is at the bottom, wearing his sister's hat but (presumably) his own pair of sunglasses. In between, the two of them are walking out along a small promontory into the River Teme in Ludlow, Shropshire.

It was the last time we were there altogether, close, before their paternal grandmother Florence died in 1997.

The painting below — the Roman figure for two and Gemini twins in symbolic combination — is by their father, one of a series Roger was painting in the late 1990s.

Then to the far right, another canvas, this time a figure that may or may not be an angel, by Hani.

They are linked, these two artworks, and curiously. So let me take you back to 2003, and a London-based gathering in the Alwyne Castle, a pub in St Paul's Road, Highbury.

Lee was turning forty and I too — back in the UK and on my way to see my mother in Scotland — had yet another reinvention/birthday in the offing, so we decided to join forces, celebrate together and try to pull together many of the people we had not seen for the fifteen plus years I had been in Japan.

It was an extraordinary mix, including friends from the distant past and those met much more recently. And no sooner had Roger gifted me his painting of my zodiac sign, which touched me deeply, than Astrid and Hani turned up — a real surprise this — and Hani shyly presented me with proof of his own talent.

I have known Astrid, born in Paraguay but a world citizen in every respect, since 1987; we met at a super-extravagant art exhibition in Tokyo during the Bubble years. It was at Seibu's flagship store in Yurakucho which, synchronistically, closed up shop just the other day.

(No, I don't believe in coincidences, nor indeed accidents.)

Astrid was working as a curator and consultant, and also represented artists, which is how we came to meet.

Invited to Hani's first show in Tokyo in 2001, I was won over by his shy and modest charm, and the deeply philosophical and mystical

nature of his work. A former Iraqi resident of Baghdad, he had been pressured by Sadam Hussein to become his official portrait painter, but instead left family and friends and fled the country.

For several years he floated around, stateless, until the UK (in its then infinite generosity and wisdom) finally gave him safe haven as a political refugee. Which is where Astrid found him, alone and struggling.

What began as a friendship and business relationship matured into respect and love, and while they are no longer together as a couple, their feelings for one another remain unchanged.

I loved his works but it was clear from the beginning that price-wise they were completely out of my league. When I asked Astrid once about one of Hani's angelic figures, she said, oh yes, there was one hanging in the Argentine Embassy in Tokyo that I could buy at a discount; I think ten thousand dollars was the figure mentioned . . .

So imagine my depth of emotion when he pressed a painting into my hands and wished me a happy day.

And so it proved to be. A very happy day.

We now need to move on smartly, because there may be some impropriety in hanging a naked woman between two men, one of whom is once again re-married and the other, Muslim.

The smallest artwork on the wall, mounted in the largest frame, is a *hanga* wood block printed in black ink on *washi* paper, and shows a woman with long hair seated on a zabuton and scribing her name with a calligraphy brush on a scroll of paper: KA-TE-RI-NA it reads as written in *katakana*, the syllabic alphabet devised as part of the Meiji reformation, to sound out all foreign words.

The main image is a nude self-portrait of Caterina, who I visited twenty years ago in the washi papermaking town of Ogawa-machi in Saitama Prefecture, north of Tokyo. A teacher in Italy, she had been given time off to come to Japan and never went back; for all she knew the Ministry of Education was still looking for her.

Admitting to an interest in erotica from an age many might judge to be exceedingly precocious, Caterina was at the time of our meeting about to leave Japan after a decade of printmaking. She had tried to leave several times before but always returned. This time her ticket was one-way.

Japan is like that: addictive.

Did she stay in Africa, which was a stop off on her way back? Did she return to Italy, face the music (if any was playing to welcome her home) and make a life there? Or did she scrimp and save to return here, drawn once again by an enigmatic culture where little shocks but rules rule and (the mythology of) total acceptance eludes.

I have no idea.

But I do like her print, which was from her farewell exhibition in May 1992: Ciao, Caterina.

I also like her quote, used to caption the photograph that accompanied the interview published in *The Japan Times* on May 3 of that year: *Japan was never a place of arrival, but always imminent departure. It's been a nice big comfortable station, to mix my metaphors, but now I want to catch another train.*

In order for us to move on, raise your eyes to the Canadian First Nation print that Nik gave us some years down the line. A dancer originally with the Royal Ballet in London and choreographer, he too had endeavoured to make his erotic mark here, but found it increasingly disconcerting and frustrating that Japan so easily both accepted and rejected everything he threw its way.

Anyone who has read Nick Bornoff's *The Pink Samurai* knows the depths to which sexual mores and behaviours are explored and exploited in this country; it's a fascinating book, but it's not pretty.

So best perhaps to concentrate upon indigenous frogs and ravens, which permeate aspects of Haida culture on the West coast of British Columbia as readily symbolic as the male phallus and female genitals do in Shinto fertility rituals throughout Japan.

A frog hangs suspended between two ravens, its limbs connected to beaks and wings; another crouches face-on between their feet. Between them I count ten eyes, which is most peculiar considering there are only four creatures, two of whom (the ravens designed side-on) show only one eye each. So where are the extra two pairs? Now I see . . . there are two faces within the bodies of the birds, facing one another.

Lifting them all down to recover their provenance (this time easy to extract as the back of the framing slots out) I find two small spiders' nests attached to the wall, as precisely placed and equidistant as the design elements of the print itself. Clever that.

Coast Salish artist Joe Wilson (signed as Joseph M. Wilson) would surely appreciate this fine example of synchronicity.

A member of the Cowichan Band near Duncan, B.C., Joe was taught to carve by his stepfather at age eleven, but was basically self-taught as a print maker. Last heard of he was living and working on the Tsartlip reserve near Victoria, where he was painting and carving cedar. Mind you, that was a fair old time ago, so I need to chase him up . . .

But as he wrote of this particular innovative screen print in 1989, produced by Pacific Editions Limited (numbered 87/100): *The design is loosely based on a spindle whorl — a tool used by the Salish for spinning wool and hair. The ravens used to decorate the whorl were indicative of spirit helpers to the spinner. The central frog in the design is similar to one that appears on an ancient stone bowl. Historically, both animals are bringers of important news. J.W.*

Unlike this print, so commercially savvy in its marketing, the lamp near the top of the wall is another of Shoi's one-offs, pure and simple. It was made from a shallow wooden dish created from short lengths of pine bound with copper, as in barrel making. In fact the English translation of *sushi oke* is sushi cask. We have one in a kitchen cupboard, used specifically for making sushi rice.

Shoi, however, has turned the basic design on its head, by piercing the sides and base for a Hokusai-style wave pattern, staining the exterior dark brown, and fitting it out as a wall lamp, with light filtering through washi paper glued to the inside.

It's very modest, very subtle.

As is the artwork below, a board bearing a screwed-in copper plate etched with a hand raised in blessing and bordered by painted and gilded hieroglyphics and universal signs and symbols.

I bought it from Beatrix, the Italian-born evolutionary astrologer/artist/yoga teacher that I consulted in Tokyo several times in the summer of 2005, before she returned with her partner Pancho to their spiritual retreat — the Nong Khai Alternative Centre — founded on the Mekong River in northern Thailand in the early 1990s.

Beatrix was profoundly helpful in casting light on the difficulties I was experiencing in understanding my mother and coming to terms with my relationship with her. She may like to know that when my mother died in 2007, we parted, I believe, as loving and forgiving friends.

I will always be grateful to Beatrix for that.

So here we are, arrived at the doorway into the next part of the house, above which hang three more pictures.

The photograph of ferns, one leaf green, t'other orange, was shot by Paul, a journalist and photo-journalist from Downunder, who worked for *The Daily Yomiuri* newspaper for almost a decade.

I was constantly stumbling across him in Hayama when we lived there, his tall rangy form bent low to shoot some tiny flower or plant with a macro-lens, dreadlocks dangling. He was hanging out and partying in a house just over the brow of the hill behind us, occupied mostly but not exclusively by Australians.

When Paul moved on, he settled in New Zealand, where he had cleverly invested in land on the picturesque west coast of the South Island, in a little town called Karamea, which is in the heart of the of the Kahurangi National Park.

There he began to create a community called the Living in Peace Project, the design of which he planned to base on the peace sign, large enough to be visible from space.

Nine years on, the Rongo project incorporates a travellers' hostel, art gallery, permaculture farm, radio station, organic food and recycled clothing shop and a motel complex . . .

As he mailed just this morning: *Sanae and I are great, thanks . . . I have my right arm in a cast after a failed stunt and we're very busy at this time of year, but everything is going rather well . . . "*

Akii and I really must go and visit sometime. We've been promising ourselves for years.

So too, to call on Demi in New Jersey, U.S.A. if we are ever that way. It is her gift that hangs next to Paul's own — a line of Indian dancers painted in exquisite detail on dark green silk.

I met Demi walking through Shibuya on my way to work at NHK (*Nippon Hoso Kyokai*, Japan Broadcasting Corporation), so it must have been a Thursday or Friday morning, for those were the days of my four-hour shifts at Japan's national broadcaster.

Apologetically requested by an Indian woman — a tourist, I assumed — to take her photograph, I was happy to oblige; talking for a few minutes, I learned she was visiting her son John, who was teaching in Japan but about to go to India to check out his mother's homeland regarding potential work in IT.

After swapping contact information and subsequently meeting up with John, I really thought no more about it. Until the following Christmas, when an enormous box turned up, stuffed with . . . well, typical American stuff like Hershey Bars and cans of baked beans, but also the most beautiful silk painting; so thoughtful to feel the need to feed me in both body and soul.

We remain in touch.

Finally, another photograph, this time of a Buddhist monk pushing open heavy wooden gates in the doorway of a temple.

Rita — an Avatar Master from Philadelphia but now in Melbourne; how people do move around these days! — brought it as an *omiyage* to a Level 2 writing class after she had spent ten days in Bhutan. She also presented the small pair of cymbals now resting on the *kamidana*, thinking I might be able to use them ritually in some way . . . and so I do.

When asked why she had chosen that particular photo for me, she smiled in reply, "Because you are opening the gates for us."

Below all these gifts is another wooden door that slides shut to the left, so making the tiny hallway that leads left to the guest room and right to the bathroom (*ofuro*) a self-contained unit.

This door is rarely used, however, featuring instead a large square panel of black fabric embroidered with two rectangles of seed-like shells and red and black thread; another Thai tribal piece.

Below which stands a small triangular Spanish cupboard in a dark wood, with a rather odd Formica top and rounded doors — a piece that Sonia no longer had room for and was found to fit our corner space perfectly.

We use it for storing bottles of (currently) brandy, gin [and tonics] and wine. For now, concentrate on this installation; we will address the major fitting in glass and wood to the right that divides the dining room from the kitchen soon enough.

On top of the Itos' cupboard (hung with a hand raised in blessing worked from tin and decorated in repoussé style with finely detailed hammering) stands a three-armed wrought-iron candlestick with a remarkable back story.

It was made in a forge in Kamakura, by a twenty-fourth-generation swordsmith — a direct descendant of the famed craftsman who signed his swords 'Masamune'.

The original Masamune was ordered to the city, possibly from Sagami Prefecture, around AD 1300. There he was instructed by the militaristic head honcho (*shougun*) of this medieval capital to create the finest swords ever made.

It is said he forged each one a thousand times (for one thousand layers) from one-hundred-year-old temple nails and iron sand from the far north, and spent eight days polishing the finished product.

Nowadays, of course, there is not such a steady demand for swords as lethal weapons, and thank goodness for that; rather they are regarded as ritual objects, or artefacts to be admired by collectors.

When visited a few years ago, Yamamura-san was sweating as he worked on a sword commissioned by a shrine in a neighbouring town; due to be interred with all due ceremony, it would quite possibly not see the light of day for a century or more. So he was anxious about making any error that might be judged in the future.

As a 'Masamune', he explained, he had a lot to live up to!

But such jobs are rare and not exactly stress-free, so he has built up a profitable sideline in creating fine-honed kitchen knives (I have two in my kitchen drawer) and decorative objects in wrought iron.

Call by the forge at the back of the shop any weekday and you may be lucky enough to see him in action, aided and abetted by *deshi* (apprentices). There is, at long last, a rising interest among young people in traditional Japanese crafts, and not all those who apply for an apprenticeship are Japanese.

Alongside our candlestick lie the three talking sticks that we use in discussion groups; if someone wants to speak they pick up a stick, so avoiding the chaos of everyone talking at once and/or losing their cool.

We can thank James, now back in California with Reiko, for that useful ruling. For the sticks also, which were picked up from the forest floor on one of Art Nature's spiritually quest-related walks, and nicely peeled.

Before stepping forward out of the dining room, keep your eyes peeled for the small round antique glass painting that hangs on the wall of the no-more-than-a-metre-deep hallway through the doorway.

See it, straight ahead? It bears (no pun intended) the image of a geisha or *maiko* (apprentice geisha) at her ablutions. She is mostly covered up but there is more than the hint of a nipple, and the whole effect is very charming

Many people fail to notice her as they head either left or right, focussed on the job in hand, but in deference we will make a little bow and turn left . . . promising to pay our respects once more as we later cross back over the tiny hallway into the bathroom area.

THE GUEST ROOM + TOILET NO. 3

yohshitsu no kyakushitsu + mittsume no toire

When we first moved into the house, this room was not happy.

It ought to have been, being bright and light, with windows on two sides providing views of the garden along the front and down the side.

But visitors were often not comfortable sleeping here, despite being supplied with a funky red sofa bed that fits into the alcove, a small free-standing wardrobe (or closet, as called here in American fashion), a rattan-crafted chest of drawers with books and a silk lamp from Burmese Myanmar on top, a fold-up table and a stool — and a wonderful spiral-stitched round rag rug speckled in red and pale blue on beige, like a bird's wing, that occupies much of the polished wood floor space.

This floor covering was carried home on my shoulder some

fifteen years ago from a community market in Hayama — one of those held seasonally in front of City Hall — having cost all of three hundred yen. (About two pounds sterling at the time. Now the exchange rate is crippling.)

What makes the room special is that it has its own separate toilet in the corner. What makes it even more popular is that this is a Western-style loo with a heated seat.

Such a clever company, TOTO, which holds a monopoly on sanitary ware in Japan, and why Europe has not caught on to such a simple joy is beyond me. Personally I would not go as far as many computerized designs do these days — going way beyond the duty of a bidet. But they always create a stir.

As for the power needed for such luxuries, Japan has too many nuclear power plants already, especially in a country with the potential for any imaginable natural disaster: earthquakes, tsunami, typhoons, blizzards, tornados, heat waves — even the equivalent of a monsoon period in summer (*tsuyu*).

Still, it has to be said: a warm seat on a cold day is immeasurably comforting, if totally unnecessary.

To add to the cheer, the walls of the toilet are painted a bright sunny yellow, sponged with white. A funky little mirror hangs off the sliding window above the toilet, with a frame created from recycled plastic bags.

Sounds horrendous? Not at all, lovely bright colours and textured like wild brush or deep carpet. It's one of Merry's early Eco Deco products, as is the Burmese lamp, now that I come to think of it.

On the narrow wall beside the toilet door, a playing card framed in black often causes comment — if noticed, that is. In general people tend not to be too observant beyond their immediate concerns.

I drew it from a pack as the finale of an act demonstrated by a young red-haired magician working the tables in the prestigious Shinjuku Park Hyatt's New York Grill back in the early 1990s. He had come to Japan to study Japanese at Waseda University and found his blissful niche in turning magic tricks. Imagine my surprise at the time to find — written in black pen across the red five of hearts — the message: I KNEW I WOULD MEET YOU HERE TONIGHT! STEVE COHEN.

Taking it down now from the wall, to check it out, give glass and frame a quick wipe, makes me wonder, for we lost touch after his article was published. For me the message was enough, can't speak for him.

And guess what! (Google turning up trumps again.) He's famous, nicknamed the Millionaire's Magician, because he performs for the stars and hosts intimate gatherings to witness his parlour tricks at the Waldorf Astoria in New York. I am so surprised; it's quite made my day.

I'm glad he is still doing what he told me he believed he was born to do: not simply entertain but raise awareness of the possibility that life operates on an infinite number of wondrous levels.

And that is it for the toilet, except for the tiny washbasin in the corner, with a strip of red tape around the drainage pipe underneath, and three tiny mirrors on the floor in the corners of the room.

Which takes me back to my first line about the guest room, and by association, its integrated toilet, being an unhappy place. Unhappy may be too strong a word. Rather, not as welcoming and comfortable as it ought to have been, location and furnishings and all other things considered. Visitors would say it was cold (when it was not) or that they felt disturbed, with strange dreams.

It was Azzah who truly raised the alarm, by reporting that she had been woken in the night by someone or something sitting on her — or rather, by the sensation or impression of being sat upon!

Which transported me even further back, to the gamekeeper's cottage in a remote valley that I used to rent on the Isle of Wight, when the children were small.

However many people came to stay, no-one would sleep in the back room on the ground floor. And it's true it felt bad — unfriendly, deathly — the very moment you opened the door. It was always like an ice-box, even when the rest of the house was warm and toasty from the log fire in the living room. The cottage had no mains electricity, only gas lights, so no TV — bliss.

John, my partner at that time, who was a great believer in ghosts and all things supernatural, hated staying there, which I guess is why we saw so little of him. I was not afraid, but rather respectful. That room in England had unfinished business in the 1970s, just as our Japanese guest room did in the early years of the twenty-first century.

The solution was clear: to clear it. Moving from corner to corner, I scattered sage and salt while instructing whatever former energy was still hanging around, to please move on: I'm sorry you are unhappy but this is our home now and it's time for you to go.

Also I borrowed Sonia's book on *fuu sui*/feng shui, and applied some of the energy-based basic principles to those areas of the house that needed adjustment. The *genkan* was one, hence the emphasis on circles and fresh water.

Our guest room/toilet — the Prosperity Room, according to the ancient Chinese tradition of building design in particular relation to the four compass points — was off to a positive start once the clearance was effected with the red sofa and other bright spiritual elements — the spiralling rug, for example).

The problem lay in the toilet. The accumulation of wealth and flushing do not go hand in hand. It had always been a bit of mystery that I was so good at making money and so useless at keeping it . . . it always flowed away from me like, well, water.

Seeking more ways to improve life in general, I placed the mirrors so as to reflect energy back upwards into the room, and always ask guests that they leave the toilet lid closed to ensure nothing energetic flows back down in that direction.

Finally, the red tape under the basin ensures that only water drains away, nothing else. And whether you believe this or not is irrelevant, because it's effective. I now have loot. Not a lot, but more than I have ever had before.

As I have said before and will without a doubt say again, whatever works . . .

The pictures on the guest room walls are simple but cheering. Two lovely paintings that Sarah and Adrian picked up while on their travels in China: one a market scene, full of hustle and bustle and detail; the other of fowl running and feeding between squash flowers and pumpkins.

To the right of the window, with a single white blind, hangs a black and white drawing of trees from a fifth floor window in South Kensington's Bina Garden, London, torn from an art pad, that Roger sent while still with Jenny; it was a lovely flat that, and

they lived there for most of Lotte's life. Lotte is Buffy and Lee's half-sister; they're all very close.

Below, a painting on some kind of animal skin of African women squatted on the ground and plaiting one another's hair, from the time Sarah was working for the World Health Organisation in

115

Kenya. Something to do with education in sanitation, I seem to recall, so the fact that the women are preening on their way to or from the toilet makes perfect sense.

On the other side of the room, left of the doorway as you enter is a photograph of Japanese queuing up to buy *tako yaki*, a cheap and popular snack of bits of octopus cooked in batter, then brushed with brown or soy sauce.

Followed by the object that has in more recent times led Kathryn to christen this, The Henry Miller Room.

She says the name came to her in May 2010, during a party to celebrate the coming of summer and yet another personal reinvention day, when she and many others, were entertaining one another, crammed into the (these days, happy, happy) guest room — which un-coincidentally is where the drinks table was situated.

Which is no doubt why on this particular day she also described the room as Wine-Soaked.

How strange this must have felt, having stayed in the room on a number of occasions and finding its atmosphere so quiet and peaceful — conducive to abstemious reclusivity, she reckoned, a bit like a monk's or nun's cell.

Henry Miller preferred to hang out in bars, however, so in a way I understand why he is here rather than any other part of the house. Maybe it's because Guest Room accepts and never judges; rather it welcomes whosoever and whatsoever enters through the door, offering its unconditional blessing.

I had trouble when I first hung Henry here, because I read his message as being so negative and angry. But that was because I was in trouble, and merely projecting. Poor Henry: he spent a year in the ground-floor *nando*, face to the wall, poor thing, all because of my own reaction. Then I read *Radical Forgiveness* by Colin Tipping and once again life was never the same; I saw Henry in a different light.

Now I can stand in front of him and acknowledge with compassion his unconsciousness, his inability to see that there was no-one standing in the way of happiness and fulfillment but himself.

A great ball-breaking writer, but never a happy man.

But I am way ahead of myself; I really must explain.

Not so long ago, you see — 2007 by the file dating — I was introduced to the Don of Roppongi.

Roppongi is an area in central Tokyo where foreign men have gone to pick up Japanese girls and drink themselves into multi-cultural bar fights since American Occupation Forces were billeted in the area after World War Two, when all kinds of bars and dance halls sprang up to cater to the so-called needs of soldiers far from home.

That honeymoon period through the post-war period into the 1960s and beyond was remembered well by Takeshi Maki, who remembers mixing with artists and intellectuals of the period and going out dancing with Yasunari Kawabata, Japan's first Nobel Prize winner for Literature.

Maki-san has had an extraordinary life.

Born in 1929 on the northern island of Sakhalin, his father disappeared in Manchuria, quite possibly arrested by the Japanese for having close links with Russia.

His mother died — also mysteriously — when he was seven, and he was shipped back alone to Hokkaido, where a rich businessman took him under his wing, put him to work in Kobe, and funded him through fashion school.

He opened a shop in Roppongi fifty years ago, with his own fashion label MK, then moved into property and antiques. He can remember five antique shops on Roppongi-dori; now there is only one, Maki's Roppongi New Gallery (formerly Roppongi Old Gallery) sited within the tall pink edifice that he built during the Bubble years.

When we met, he was simplifying, realizing his assets with a single purpose in mind — to lay his fortune on the table towards Peace in Asia. He believes the Korean peninsula ought to be an integrated neutral zone.

As he showed me around his still jam-packed emporium, we stopped on the picture-hung staircase, where I questioned the origin of a framed series of existential questions and statements in various coloured inks in English and French.

Ah, Maki-san explained: the American writer Henry Miller — who together with his fifth wife, the Japanese jazz singer Hoki Tokuda, ran a club called Tropic of Cancer in Maki's basement — used to dash off scribbles and pictures in lieu of rent. This apparently was the last in his possession.

At the time I was not sure . . . for one thing, the signature was Henry Valentine, not Miller. But, as I learned later, Valentine was his middle name, and he liked to use it to keep people (like me) guessing.

A week later the artwork turned up in Zushi, a gift, Maki-san

said, for a job well done and because I had responded so vigorously and knew who Miller was. You'd be surprised, he noted, how many people have never heard of him!

The piece is headed in a nice firm looping hand, but from thereon — as follows in the style in which it's laid out — the message is all downhill:

From the Halls of Monteguma

A la bas Noel **[in black ink]**
(Down with Christmas!) **[red ink]**
Merde a vous tous! **[in black)**
(to hell with all of you!) **[red, and so on]**
Tous moi, la paix!
(Fuck off!)
No X'mas on Earth,
This year or the next.

(tsch, tsch, tsch!)
No peace, no joy,
(rien que rien)
no, nothing.
At 87, still a fool,
but no longer God's own
fool. Somehow, somewhere
the devil has crept in.
le sous signe
C'est moi qui le dit.
Henry Valentine

Down the left-hand side [in green]:
In
my
palace
of
memory
there
is
only
you.
(what luck!)
La vie
est drole,
n'est ce
pas?
Quo
Vadis,
ou
est vous?

Down the right-hand side [also in green]:

Love

is

like

a

melody

(in

what

key?)

It makes no. . .

never

mind!

La

vrai

vie

est

absent.

Et

toi

aussi. . . .

It is interesting that the overall effect is so carefully patterned, when he was so obviously eaten up with anger and frustration. But he was a painter as well as a novelist, so as sharp and deliberate with design as with words.

Despite the furious need to express his despair over his decade-long relationship with Tokuda (who apparently refused to sleep with him), he still maintained a literary stance, changing languages and pens to stylistically holistic effect. Only the slip with the spelling of Montezuma seems out of place, but he was surely under pressure, and how many celebrities when asked to scribble an autograph or message bother to proofread?

(Same with e-mails and IT communications in general these days.)

Miller lived another decade, dying in 1980 at age eighty-nine. During which time he fell in love at least once more, stirring further outpourings of emotionally loaded letters. Dignity had nothing to do with anything in his old age; eroticism and passion were all, and kept him in thrall.

On that birthday in May last year, Kathryn gifted me an anthology of those letters he wrote to Tokuda; she had found it in a second-hand bookshop in her stamping ground of Tokyo's Shimokitazawa.

Such kindness, so thoughtful.

It stands now among the small collection assembled for guests, and while not having pride of place — because Heather's book on Kamakura is there, together with titles by Duncan in Orkney, even my insider title on Tokyo — it most certainly holds its own.

THE BATHROOM
ofuro

One giant step across the hallway, past the lovely Japanese lady baring a perfect boob, and we are through the small *noren* (woven in *asa*, flax, and dyed in *ai*, indigo) bought in Noboribetsu two decades ago, and into the bathroom, or rather the undressing-dressing room that leads into the *ofuro* proper.

It's a small, square, cream-painted room with shelves and cupboards for towels and cosmetics, these latter held in baskets that slide in and out, one for Akii, one for me. Also a glass-fronted cabinet that slides underneath, for hair dyes (red, pink and mango predominate) and nightclothes, toasty flannel in winter, light cotton pants and T-shirts in summer.

The only non-utilitarian object? A brightly painted fishing boat, bought on Orkney when visiting Ingrid and Duncan. We had gone over to Hoy on the ferry, and Ingrid (accompanied by her small daughter, Cara) led us to a garage where a local man created all manner of naïve but beautifully crafted toys and objects out of driftwood and offcuts.

Ahoy! (as she was instantly nicknamed) has been sailing the world ever since.

Below the window is a wide stainless steel sink, formed out of a single piece of metal, with a large corked glass bottle of soaps, and mugs for toothbrushes. Small towels hang off metal swing bars, airing when the window is slid open.

Below is a cupboard, again with sliding doors, which houses cleaning stuff and — in summer — the usual infestation of ants and even cockroaches, known unaffectionately as *gokiburi*.

The latter are part and parcel of living in Japan, especially outside the city and in an older house, and while initially they would upset me a lot, now I simply ask that they stay in their space and respect my own. Not so simple in August, when they tend to run havoc and have been known to use the corridor between the *genkan* and dining room as a racetrack. But I smile fondly (while clenching my teeth) and look the other way.

On the wall behind, behind the door into the space, is a mirror, below which is a rail for towels, and above, a framed photograph of a wintry snow-blown beach in Chigasaki, looking towards Izu and the Hakone foothills of Japan's most sacred mountain, Fuji-san.

Beautifully spare, it is the work of a young Japanese photographer who, sadly, I failed to keep up with (and she with me). I met her in 2000 on Omote-sando in Tokyo, where she was selling her work on the pavement. I recall she had travelled all over the world on her own, which was still rare in those days; also her pleasure that I liked this particular picture because it reminded me of my early days in Japan.

There are other pictures too: on the creamy door into a cupboard

(with another mirror inside) are two tiny pieces, one oil on board, of Isshiki beach in Hayama, dated in pencil in Japanese to the Taisho period (1912–1926), above a contemporary watercolour framed in blue of the canals and warehouses in Otaru, purchased on a working trip to Hokkaido in the mid-1990s.

There are also two larger canvasses in oil, say A-3 size, of seascapes — one full of light, the other showing a dark jade curling wave — found in a long-gone pawn shop in Zushi. I think they cost five hundred yen each.

Our dressing gowns hang on pegs, thick fleece in winter (it can be very cold) and cotton *yukata* in summer. The black and white mat on the polished wooden floor in front of the sink is a baby brother to that in the corridor; the one we put down for when bathing is recycled from a lovely thick green towel that had begun to fray at the edges. It is absolutely typical of me to be buying expensive while making do and mending — going from one extreme to another.

Sliding open the glass doors into the bathroom proper always comes as a surprise to guests. Wow, they say, it's huge! And (double wow) a garden!

Huge? Well, larger than many, but then many Japanese ofuro are not much larger than the bath tub itself, with only just enough space to scrub down, rinse off, climb in and out.

Our own is bizarre in that it has a small door on the far side, to the right of the tub, which comes out opposite the kitchen door . . . the kind of mini-door for entering humbly into a room designed for the tea ceremony, though why you would need to bow low in order to get clean remains beyond my capacity for cultural comprehension.

The bathroom ceiling is lined with planks of sealed pine. The walls are tiled in pink. Not my style at all . . . Japan has ruined me for this lovely colour, obsessed as it is with Kitty-chan, princesses and all things Disneyesque.

The floor is pebbled in blue and pink and dark green; sounds weird for sure, but for some odd reason it works, and I'm more than used to it.

The synthetic tub itself, set into the floor so that when filled and heated and you step in and sit down you are up to your neck in lovely hot water, is cream-coloured, matched with a stirrer (for mixing the water to a bearable temperature) and a stool and basin for washing and scrubbing. There is also a simple shower, with mixer taps.

Standing under the generous spray of water and thanking my lucky stars for such luxury, I often think of my mother these days, and how she loved her English bath . . . her idea of bliss being to lie in several inches of scummy water until it turned cold.

Japanese would turn in their collective graves. They consider such a habit dirty, impure, preferring to wash and rinse first, and only then, when every patch of skin and crack and crevice is scoured bright pink, to climb into piping hot clean water and relax: dream, meditate, read, create, drink hot sake or ice-cold beer (depending on the season), chat with friends (if the bath is big enough, which it invariably is in commercial ofuro and *onsen* (hot springs) and generally just hang out, therapeutically speaking.

I love my tub. I love it especially because it faces floor-to-ceiling sliding glass windows onto a small patch of green enclosed by a high wall, so private.

I was going to say totally private, but this was proved wrong last year when workers cut down all the trees and vegetation on the hillside outside, so providing themselves with a clear view of all our comings and goings. But they are long gone, and thanks to chants and prayers, and Nature's immense fortitude, much is growing back.

Akii likes to bathe in illuminated neon. I prefer to put the light on in the garden and switch off those inside, so I can watch the changing of the seasons, the movement of stars across the sky.

Just the other day, there was a full moon. The massive tree in the neighbour's garden below that usually hides the sky in summer with a canopy of leaves, is budding but still skeletal, so the view was unimpeded, very clear.

In autumn the colours are lovely, and I do not count winter as having arrived for sure until a certain leaf on a topmost branch has finally blown away. Soon, though, it now being spring, there will be new bamboo shooting for the sky, and in early summer, hydrangeas. Also there are pots full of geraniums, programmed to start flowering pink, white, red and plum-coloured any day now . . .

Yes, I love my tub.

Even when scrubbing it — and the rest of the bathroom — down, which I do stark naked.

For then I feel doubly cleansed, inside and out.

THE KITCHEN
daidokohro

It's hard to say where the kitchen starts and finishes, complicated as it is by a bar-come-hatch that divides the cooking area by three-quarters across the dining room, with an open doorway in the final quarter.

You come out of the entrance between the guest room and bathroom area, with Beatrix's handy blessing to the right, and that lovely embroidered Thai hanging and triangular Spanish cupboard to the left, and look through into the kitchen to the sink, draining board and stove with windows above on the far side.

The lower and top halves of the dividing structure are made up of wooden cupboards above and below. In between (on the dining room side) is an opening with shelves and sliding doors of plate glass; from the other side — from inside the kitchen — the doors are wooden, so cutting the area in half if required. It never is ... has never been closed off to date. And, while there is a first time for everything, I foresee no reason why things will not remain just as they are.

Many things are stood inside the cupboard, some facing the dining room area, others the kitchen. Photos (of Lee with my mother, Buffy on her wedding day, Akii and I at the Oasis *umi no ie* (literally, sea house), a favourite summer beach bar; ceramics (antique and modern); *urushi* lacquerware (old and new, Thai and Japanese); glasses (wine and water); any number of small vessels for consuming sake (no two alike); a pair of English tea cups and saucers (for English tea-drinking guests); bowls containing coinage from various trips abroad; a small blown glass vase for flowers (one of Joy's creations), a sake jug containing a dried branch that Julia brought as a gift when she was around four; so many things, each with its own original and (to me) important story.

The small brass figure of Shiva is special: god of the yogis (so self-controlled and celibate) but also destroyer of the world, responsible for change both in the form of death and the shedding

of ego, meaning false identification with form and including saying good riddance to old habits and attachments. (Like all this stuff in my head, my house . . .)

Talking of which, my miniature Buddhist monk, carved from ivory and seated on a *zabuton*, toes pointing neatly forward and hands together, praying, also has a special place in my heart. I found him in, of all places, a Scottish church-turned-antique emporium in Dunkeld, Perthshire, back in the early 1990s.

Asked if they had anything Japanese, I was led to a small cupboard containing a few dusty *netsuke* and fans. About to turn away, I caught sight of this tiny figure in hiding in a dark corner. Oh, come out, I thought; time you went home!

He was very expensive, I seem to recall. And I have no idea of his provenance, with only the two kanji for *yama-kawa* (mountain-river) carved into the base as guidance. Many times I have thought of contacting an antiques show on Japanese TV, but never got around to it. Possibly he is two a yen or maybe he's a rarity of great value. Whichever, we'll never be parted, unless exactly the right time and occasion presents itself.

Some of these items — I am no "collector", as such, and hate to believe I go in for knick-knacks, but I guess many would describe them so — are displayed on the glass shelf, supported on a single unfixed metal rod. Every time I dust (which is not very often) my heart is in my mouth that the whole fragile edifice will come tumbling down. Yet it survives Julia in her wildest moments of hurtling past, and even major earthquakes and minor tremors; quite remarkable really.

So too is the endurance of the *noren* curtain that hangs in the kitchen doorway. Woven from natural cotton and illustrated with a stem of bamboo in firm but delicate black and grey brushstrokes, it dates from my earliest days here, having hung now in three different homes.

How many times has it gone through the twin tub? True, it is beginning to wear a little thin, but continues to carry and reflect our history with beauty and style, being never happier than when in Hayama, where we were surrounded by bamboo, and the design told everyone who entered the *genkan* where it hung the name of the house: *take no uchi*, bamboo house.

So, the kitchen . . .

Japanese friends tend to say it is large. By contrast, visitors from abroad are often shocked — and some may even pity me — thinking it primitive. After all, I have no stove, only two gas rings. Yet in twenty-five years it has never caused us to go hungry; quite the opposite.

Indeed, Christmas last, we fed neighbours and writers from far and wide with nine courses, including cream of (five different types of) mushroom soup, a variety of vegetables and chicken (or fish) with spiced red pepper puree, and Christmas pudding and white brandy sauce. Just a matter of patience, juggling and teamwork, none of which I was especially good at in the past, but

seem to have draped over my shoulders here like an acquired cultural cloak.

The large pale-grey American-size fridge was adopted from Catherine and Graham when they left; it still has their stickers on, I realize, and pledge to do something about that!

Alongside stands a steel shelving unit with rice cooker and bags of rice (polished [white, *kome*] and unpolished [brown, *genmai*]) on the top shelf, a bread bin on the second together with plastic boxes of pulses and pasta (which then extend down onto the shelf below) and at the bottom, cutting boards and a large glass jar containing . . . what? eggs, potatoes, fruit?

'Ping Pong!' Plums. Very ancient plums, dating from when I was living in Chigasaki in the late 1980s.

I had become quite excited by unusual seasonal activities centred around foodstuffs and decided to try and make *umeshu* (plum wine), which I knew to be pleasantly efficacious. (I was still drinking a lot in those days.) So off to the supermarket I went and returned loaded with jars, green plums, rock sugar, and *shochu* (rice liquor). Just a matter of throwing everything in, filling it up, screwing on the red cap and settling in to wait.

Six weeks later, with Akii away at work in Yokohama, I tested and yay! I tested and tasted again, delicious. Again: even better. Several glasses later I began to feel not simply drunk and dizzy but really quite ill. . . and may in fact have passed out. I know it took days to recover and since then, I have been unable to smell umeshu without feeling sick. A pity no-one had thought to warn me that it was so strong, so potentially lethal in large doses.

Now I am wondering why I still have the jar — time to throw it out?

Definitely time for them to go. Going . . . going . . . gone!

Take care by the open doorway; there's a foot-high step down onto concrete. That funny little door from the bathroom is on the left, a door leading outside to the right, and straight ahead, a deep pit, which may once have housed a water tank or heating system. Now a twin-tub washing machine stands perched on boards above the space; one of Akii's improvisations. A *noren* made from vintage fabric striped in greyish green and white hangs in front in a vague attempt to hide it from view.

The stainless steel sink unit and stove, on top of a cupboard storing toilet rolls, are under the window, which looks out onto the concrete-clad hillside behind the house.

There are three wire baskets on the wide steel-clad window shelf: cat food in one; washing up stuff in the one in the middle; metal cooking implements in that to the right.

Lots of bits and bobs — a jar of Pommery mustard, containers (metal disguised as wood and plastic) for green tea (*ocha*), tins of English Breakfast, Earl Grey, even Lapsang Souchong (when I can find it), a clear jar with a blue glass lid for brown sugar, a hand-thrown bowl with blue patterning for onions and garlic.

Also, a collection of mugs on a wooden stand (Christmas-gifted long ago by my mother, who had exactly the same design in her kitchen in Scotland); and a lot of teapots, seven to be exact. One is glass, for home-grown herb tea in summer. Three are for green tea . . . why so many?

Two were gifted by Glen, when he gave up his English-style tea shop at Temple View in Akiya: the smallest, brown and elegantly retro-deco in style; the other a boldly-rounded cream-slipped job with a crenellated upper rim, and an applied dragonfly on one side, standing on its own square ceramic footplate.

The last — the seventh — is the one we use daily. Simply cast in aluminium (yes, I know, but are we dead yet? no), it was Made in Thailand many moons ago. Every year or so, the handle falls off. No matter. I simply screw it back on again.

The right-hand wall has a narrow plate-glass shelf for herbs and spices, below which, next to the gas rings, the metal counter top bears a larger wire basket filled with condiments — oils, vinegars, bottles of soy sauce, Thai Nam Pla (the fish sauce that smells almost as bad as durian fruit, but cooks like a dream) — and a small electric grill for making toast and heating anything small enough to fit in.

There is a Japanese pot, originally for fermenting mashed-up soya beans for *miso*, jam-packed with wooden spoons and chopsticks for whipping up eggs or cooking, and purloined/rescued from the garden of a house being demolished in Ogigayatsu.

Saucepans, frying pans and woks are stored in the cupboard below. (For "stored", read "thrown into".)

The rest of the wall is all cupboard, again in three sections: the top part with sliding wooden doors painted cream like the rest of the space; the central part with two ribbed glass doors; the lower part similar to the top.

I hesitate to open any of them, or say too much about the contents because everything is so disorganised. But the crockery has some memories to evoke, tales to tell — the five small stoneware plates with tweaked edges and as tough as they come from a kiln at Miyajima port in Hiroshima Prefecture, for example.

I was on my way back from Hiroshima after covering the Asian Games (XII Asiad) for *Asia Magazine* in the autumn of 1994, and in a detour to visit Itsukushima Shrine on the island, bought them near the ferry crossing.

Also the remnants of another set of five plates — only one still intact, the other with a large chip but used all the same — dating to the Edo-period (1603-1868) and decorated blue on white with roosters.

I bought these from a tiny antique shop in Shirahama Onsen in Wakayama Prefecture on a much later trip, after checking out an extraordinary hotel — the Kawakyu — built (with cost at the time seemingly an irrelevant bottomless pit) on the coast as homage to personal taste and integrity, and international craftsmanship: Italian mosaics, Venetian glass, British brickwork, and Barry Flanagan golden hares atop a yellow roof tiled by the same kiln in Beijing that sealed China's Forbidden City against climatic elements, if not political.

The power behind this extraordinary family project later invited me to her son's wedding, again in Hiroshima.

I have been to four weddings in Japan and this was by far the most lavishly eccentric: set on a mountain top with breath-taking views, the bride and groom (now divorced) arriving by coach and horses, and at least one guest (from the other Iranian royal family and one-time manager of the Harry Winston store in Ginza's Hotel Seiyo) by helicopter. Or did I make all that up? I know she wore riding gear with a top hat and a long floating veil; very stylish. Really, I must ask her.

I heard from Goli not so long ago via Facebook; we had shared a guest room together at the wedding and sporadically kept in touch over the years. She moved in a very different world to my own, but we liked one another, respected one another's differences and choices. Now she has a child and lives in America. I'm very happy for her.

The Kawakyu is today described, sadly, as a Resort Hotel — a non-committal term (covering a multitude of sins as well as virtues) if ever there was one. Another signature dream that went ape-shit in the Bubble collapse of the early 1990s!

Yasue — Wonder Woman, Japan-style — has had a hard time, but survives. From an old family in Nara, Japan's first recorded capital, her constant soul-searching and resilience is to be admired. If her amazingly creative entrepreneurial spirit has a motto, it surely has to be, "Never give up".

Personally, in more plebeian fashion, I will never give up on trying to return our butcher's block table (on casters, so a moveable feast) to its original pristine condition. All that carefully applied beeswax — smooth on, smooth off — has come to nothing, and now the top is as stained and battered as everything else. Very *wabi sabi* (wabi meaning 'humble', and sabi, 'the passage of time'), this being very much a point to view rather than a design feature.

Roberto made it for us — a wonderful job.

The only other surface also at waist height is the hatch counter top, which on this side, at this particular moment in time, carries a turned wooden bowl containing fruit (two red Fuji apples, two lemons — one fresh, the other desiccated to the point of mummification), one healthy-looking orange and one rather tired banana), and two piles of serving plates and bowls, plus a short stretch of cookery books that I love to read but never ever use.

From the ceramics, I choose just two: the funky bowl with chunks carved out of the surface made by a potting enthusiast in his kiln in the back of his garden behind our house in Hayama; he used to have a sale every spring and I well remember buying this piece, because he nodded sagely and said, *"Omodeto gozaimasu"* (congratulations), meaning I guess that he thought I had chosen well.

Normally, he went to work every day in a company suit, his throat chakra strangled with a neat tight tie; on this one special day of the year, when he could allow his real self free rein, he was always in indigo-dyed *samue* (traditional working clothes), with a *tenugui* cloth tied around his head, looking every part the artist craftsman.

The small white plate with a red-headed crane (*tanchoh-tsuru*) in relief, with only its head and part of a wing painted, was a survivor of the Great Hanshin Earthquake of January 17, 1995.

The major tremor that focussed most of its devastating impact on Kobe at 5:46am, woke me in Hayama just seconds before it struck, when suddenly the window banged and the glass shook and reverberated in the frame. I remember thinking, Oh, an

earthquake, and big, but not here! then going back to sleep. Only in the morning did we realize the enormity of what had happened.

Six weeks later I travelled to Kobe to write a story for *Asia Magazine* about the impact on the city and how residents were picking up the pieces.

I got the official story from the city office, and then wandered the streets in a state of ever-deepening distress, for I had not seen catastrophe on this scale since growing up in Coventry after the bombings of November 1940. I was not born when the bombs fell, but I lived with the physical and psychological devastation caused throughout my childhood.

A favourite game, for example, was walking on blackened timbers across gaping basement floors. (My parents would have died if they had known.)

Walking in Kobe along streets where buildings leaned at crazy angles, or hung perilously over cracked roads and pavements, or through back roads where jam jars of flowers in still smoking ruins indicated where people had died, was beyond moving — it was heart-breaking.

Passing one house that still stood but with the roof half gone, I noticed a small pile of plates at the front door with a hand-written For Sale notice. Picking out the one with the crane, which symbolizes happiness and longevity, I left a *sen-en* (one-thousand-yen) note.

Now all these years later I am wondering why I did not simply leave the money, and the plate. After all, it was all someone had left. It is a change of consideration in me that I am glad to note. But I still feel bad and always offer a blessing when this small remnant of Japanese history and someone's daily life is put to use.

Pass now through the noren into the dining room and round to the other side of the hatch. What is on the countertop here?

A landline phone sitting on a small piece of tribal weaving in orange and green-dyed wool, picked up in Mendoza, Argentina, on my way back by bus from Chile's Santiago to Buenos Aires in November 1999.

A small Muji writing pad and biro for messages, and the school exercise book in which I sometimes leave messages for Rika (and she to me).

One of Jill's eccentrically slipped mugs containing pens and pencils. Her biannual exhibition at Keio Department Store in Shinjuku is due in 2012. But hopefully I will see her before then on one of my trips back to London.

Then towards the far end, two boxes of Angel Cards (the first bought at Findhorn, Scotland, in 2009), incense sticks, a pack of playing cards bearing a travel map of central London, homeopathic 'No Jet Lag' pills ('The Perfect Travel Companion'), and a plastic box containing a variety of medications: some, like evening primrose oil, natural in origin; others, like the anti-inflammatory, generically synthetic.

Finally, a bottle of red wine which I bought last weekend from our local boutique wine store One.D, because it was a Malbec but which turns out on closer inspection — and with perfect synchronicity — to hail from Tupangato, Mendoza, a major wine-growing region and one I passed through on my way back from Chile to Argentina.

Some pinned-up artworks provide their own colourful stories: a thank-you note from Max for the DVD I sent him for Christmas (*Train the Dragon*), also crayon drawings of Akii and myself by Mone (Rika's daughter), and a funny pencilled cat from Julia.

It is the thought of Christmas that makes me look up, remembering that the box of decorations is packed away again back in the top cupboard; this last year-end was the first time they had been brought out in years.

Stepping out into the corridor, I turn one last time to acknowledge Leesa's bamboo collage, hanging as it does on the end of the hatch facing this part of the house.

But there is something else also — a small signed watercolour of a poppy gifted by David Reynolds, 1993.

Then a professor at UCLA School of Public Health, University of Southern California School of Medicine, and the University of Houston, David was in Tokyo to advocate Constructive Living, a Western approach to mental health education based in large part on adaptations of two Japanese psychotherapies, Morita Therapy and Naikan Therapy.

Now a published author, all his ideas and teachings have converted into a self-paced and self-directed learning system called eMods. Back then, however, in simpler pre-IT days, he was simply concerned with helping others approach life realistically, thoughtfully, and with a degree of humour.

He most certainly helped me.

In part it was the way he tackled his own deep-seated fear of flying by spending every flight painting postcards, mini-artworks that he then gave away to people met on his travels — people like me. How constructive is that!

But his approach to life also helped get a handle on my own hang up with blame. Back then I was still tending to blame my parents for just about everything that I thought had ever gone wrong with my life.

When I told David this he just looked at me, smiled quizzically and asked if I had ever counted how many times my mother had cooked my meals, washed and ironed my clothes, and how many times my father had set off to the job I knew he had always hated, simply because they loved me and my sister and our family.

I cannot over-estimate the effect those few words had on me, eighteen years ago.

After much work and reflection (which includes close attention paid to *Radical Forgiveness,* that mind-blowing book by the English writer Colin Tipping), blame is no longer a word in my vocabulary.

But wait. What about the linoleum on the kitchen floor, the

lino that I have been complaining about for the last eight years? It was battered and bruised when we first arrived; now add grossly stained to the list. Warm-looking I grant you, being a warm dark orange flecked with some colour or another (hard to tell right now). But the *yukashita-shuuno* (literally, 'storage under the floor') in the middle of the lino makes it hard to replace as a DIY job. It has a square double-door that lifts off, half by half) to reveal . . . a not-so-secret hidey hole.

After parties, when there is often beer and wine (and masses of food) leftover due to Japanese generosity, it has been useful in the past. But these leaner days, it is no longer used for anything; buying food mostly day-by-day and with both us drinking less and less, we rarely have anything to store. Nor, most certainly, anything to hide.

The two brass handles that swing upwards to lift open the doors, are buggers with agendas of their own. Many is the time I have walked across in bare feet or socks and screamed as they swung unfairly into snappy action.

Unfairness is easy to blame, so sometimes I forget and curse the architects, the builders, the owners, Akii for not doing anything about such recalcitrant joints, to reduce stubbed toes. Then I calm down and move into self-flagellatory mode, blaming myself.

Finally — and we are talking seconds here, not hours or even days — I remember David, and put blame firmly in its place — in never-never land.

THE STAIRCASE
kaidan

I have known some staircases in my time. Some very grand, others decidedly less so.

I guess the step (or two) up into the caravan my parents rented in the 1950s in Brixham, Devon, and another near Barmouth in Wales, do not count.

Which makes the single rise above the cupboard under the stairs (complete with gas masks and a genuine upright Hoover) in our 1930s semi-detached in Coventry, my first staircase of any significance.

But it was straightforward compared to my aunt and uncle's in Stourbridge, which rose in honour of its even more conservative householders and then turned very positively to the left as if to make me welcome.

Aged eleven, I was introduced to what I considered to be a magnificent sweep in my Aunt Jo's new home in Perthshire, Scotland; she had married a Scottish laird and Forneth House not only had a generously wide and carpeted staircase inside, but a marvellously decorative wrought iron affair down the outside onto the terraced part of the garden, with an aspect over Clunie Loch. Very *Gone With The Wind*, I considered. Not that I knew a thing about Atlanta, a fact that remains constant to this day.

In 1959 I left home (for the first time but not the last) to become a student, and fell in love with Bretton Hall College of Music, Art and Drama, affiliated as it was back then with Leeds University.

The house — dating from around 1720, though there was reputedly an earlier building on the site — is still there, plus the five-hundred acres of grounds, lakes and parkland through which we roamed as students as if we'd arrived in heaven. Sadly, it closed as the college I knew in 2001, and as a university campus in 2009.

There was some talk of its being turned into a spa. Now it seems that the Yorkshire Sculpture Park, which evolved from the pioneering education ethos of Bretton Hall, *a hive of creativity where artists and educators learned by doing,* is taking over.

What I remember learning to do, nose in the air to disguise a deep lack of self-confidence, was float superciliously up and down the wide staircase that rose elegantly and then divided into two, with balconies that ran around the full length of the imposing hallway, or pose equally self-consciously to sing carols at Christmas.

There was a wondrously romantic stone spiral staircase in the small chateau in France where I worked as an au pair the summer I left college. Magic.

Then two steps down into the miserable backroom bedsit in Cricklewood, where I began life in London — so cold and damp in the terrible winter of 1962 that the wallpaper was hanging off the walls! The author and poet Clive James was lodging upstairs with a gang of fellow newly-arrived clump-footed Australian 'Grillos' (our nickname for them, I'm ashamed to say, for being from far warmer climes they must have been feeling especially under the weather).

Later there was an elegant if arty five-storey house just off Kensington High Street — lots of stairs — on loan from the artist Jo Tilson and his family, who were in-residence in New York. When they came back for a term, John, Jack, Roger, me and baby Lee decamped to a first-floor flat in Paddington until the house was relinquished again for the remainder of the academic year — not so many stairs, but hell with a small child in a pram.

The stairs down into the basement in Brook Green were also tough to negotiate with a pushchair and I was pregnant again; as if to rub salt into the wound of poverty while feeding a passion for eccentricity, the bath was in the kitchen!

But then we moved to Kilburn where Lee and Buffy perfected their own climbing techniques on the concrete stairs that took us up into the first floor flat. Amazing that no one fell down the stairwell during the decade we were there.

When we moved to the Victorian terraced house I bought in Queen's Park in 1977 (not half as posh then as it is now) they had stairs to climb inside, and carpeted.

Quite the luxury.

Then I came to Japan.

When I was introduced to the four flights of filthy, litter-strewn concrete stairs of the block in the *danchi* housing estate where Akii lived then, I could only think, What on earth have I done, selling up the beautiful home and garden I had created, and leaving for this?

Such was my state of shock that I fell down the one tiny step into the *ofuro* and had to live with both bruising and sensory dislocation for weeks.

But as in every re-birthing, things improved: only one step out of the garden in Kamakura, up into our tiny one-floor tea house.

Then stone stairs outside and a single sharp flight of shiny wooden interior stairs in Hayama — the incline so extreme that when ambulance men once had to carry me down, the stretcher was near vertical and they had one man at the bottom trying to stop me sliding down and falling off.

Now, here we are:

These are also shiny wooden stairs, but gentler and wider, with rounded handrails that make climbing up and down as safe as houses, and a mezzanine halfway up, half-carpeted with a small vegetable-dyed Afghan kilim bought from a pop-up shop in Jiyuugaoka, west Tokyo.

The window at this point is enormous, or relatively so — with white folding louvre shutters that unlike *amado* we never use, and looking out onto a concrete wall covered in summer with Virginia creeper.

Unfortunately Tora adores rushing up and down this staircase— her morning exercise after being fed — leaving a legacy of scratch marks that make us quite anxious about how to explain the state of the floors if and when we ever leave. Occasionally she takes the halfway corner too sharply from upstairs and skates, crashing down the remaining flight to land ignominiously on her head.

I, on the other hand, did things in reverse.

It was moving-in day in 2002 and I was being too busybusybusy for my own good. Coming out of the living area, I forgot there was a step and launched into space, smashing face forward down across the corridor onto the lower steps of the stairs opposite.

Dazed and appalled at my own carelessness, I was pretty sure I had done some real damage. But no — simply another life used up and more bruises. (Not many lives left, Angela, if any!)

Julia grew up on these stairs. With no staircase in her own single-storey home nearby, she learned to climb on them, slowly at first but then with rapidly increasing confidence. Once she could stand she liked to play with the light switches — so annoying at times!

She learned also to count on them in English. I would hold her hand and we would go up and down one by one . . . 1, 2, 3, 4, 5, 6, 7, rest, then 1, 2, 3, 4, 5, 6, 7.

Two sets of seven; no wonder this is a lucky house.

TOILET NO. 4

yottsume no toire

Julia used to call it the star toilet, and I can quite see why, even though there is not a single star as such (neither five- nor six-pointed) to be seen. The theme is more metaphysical, but she is on the right track.

The door is on the right at the top of the stairs, with a corridor that replicates the one below on the ground floor (first floor in Japan) leading to the left.

There is a small illustration taped in place for visitors and guests, showing it to be a Western toilet but old-style, with the cistern high — the kind guys up to no good used to hide guns inside in old gangster movies — and the handle to flush hanging down on a chain.

In fact the sanitary ware itself is computerized, with buttons to press to wash various bits and pieces, and a heated seat, as in the guest room. We turn this off in summer but in mid-winter do find such comfort very seductive.

The outside of the door is faced with wood veneer as are all opening and some sliding doors upstairs and downstairs; inside is painted white, with a half-brush stroke in azure blue encircling the chrome handle, for *maru* (circle).

There is a near fully circular (*marui*) brush stroke around the small white glass lamp on the ceiling. And again the image is spontaneous and open to interpretation — life, the world, the universe . . .

In Japan, boats and ships are always the something-maru, and sometimes it is tagged onto the end of boys' names, but why? Akii — a man who likes history and words and is exceedingly literate — took it upon himself to do some research and found that maru dates from the Heian Period (794–1185) when it was a popular appellation among the elite, and also a word used to describe something precious. Boats were precious to fishermen and sea-going traders so it was added to the name in the same way.

The roots of language are so interesting, don't you think?

The floor and walls up to the halfway point are tiled in white. The sanitary ware is also white, the toilet sited below the window and a small washbasin in the corner to the right if sitting down; the door is on the left.

Above the tiling the walls are plaster-boarded, held in place with rusted nails. What to do with these, I wondered, when repainting a few years ago.

The solution was to paint the walls and ceiling bright acid yellow, and then make a small impromptu blue cross over each rust mark that showed through. Hence the starry effect.

Above the window are two spirals, also in blue. Spirals loom large in my imagery, my cyclical view of the world in the snail shell, the sea shell, the cobweb . . . The colour is repeated on the narrow window sill, on which stand toilet rolls and a cactus. Why a cactus? I don't even like cacti especially. Maybe a gift . . .

As to how it found a home in the toilet, I have no idea.

That's it really, apart from a small towel on a chrome rail by the basin. Today it is blue, but sometimes red, just to stir things up a little. Nothing else, cleaning stuff apart. No pictures. No books. Nothing to while away the time . . .

But that's me. I know other people spend a lot of time in their toilets, with magazines and newspapers and *manga* comic books, cuddly toys and bottles of wine, but I am in and out and no hanging about. Says a lot psychologically, I am sure. But then I have no problem in admitting that I never have been very anally inclined, especially in terms of holding onto anything that needs to be got rid of in order to move forward.

Looking at these words just tapped-tapped-tapped into place, I begin to wonder: am I writing about this house, our home, in preparation to letting it all go, moving on?

Upon enquiry, many friends find toilets simply good places to escape to, and I admit to using it for more than a few minutes of peace when Lee and Buffy were small. I may even have taken a book with me on occasion, desperate for some space, to be left alone.

But I could never stand the guilt for long.

Four little hands knocking on the door calling "Mummy, mummy . . . " would tug my youthfully impatient, but essentially deeply loving heart-strings every time.

THE TATAMI ROOM + STORE ROOM NO. 2
washitsu no heya + futatsume no nando

At the top of the stairs, the toilet to your right, step across into the *tatami* room — the BIG tatami room. Because here we have two rooms in one, divided by removable screen doors but with a built-in decorative opening (*ranma*) above so that air and sound circulate freely in between. It is the thing I love most about traditional Japanese architecture — its flexibility.

This room — the larger space, where we sleep — is laid with eight tatami; the other — next door — six. The *tokonoma* and then *oshiire* (for storing bedding) and the small *nando* are all here, lined up to the right, against the outside wall.

There is a pile of indigo-dyed *zabuton* in the art alcove, gifted from Nonaka-san who lives next door, possibly because she got fed up with us borrowing her own for the *rakugo* performance

that Akii stages every May as part of Golden Week, a string of consequtive national holidays that for many offers the longest holiday period in the year. (Not this year, though; our hearts were not in it.)

Also an early earthenware pot from Yuko — made after her trip to Mali with Aja Addy — very simple and inscribed with a repeating pattern of what appear to be stick insects.

Aja was a Ghanaian musician — a wizard on the talking drum — who was based in Berlin but loved Japan so much that he came every summer to tour and hang out at the beach bar Oasis on Morito Beach, teaching and playing.

He died there, very suddenly, in 2006, of a massive heart attack.

The aftershock was immense and the local community much affected. The hardest part for those directly involved was sending him home, his wife refusing to believe he was dead until she could see his physical body. Even now, when Oasis opens for the summer season in mid-July, there is a small shrine to his memory, with photos, candles to light and incense . . . Aja is much loved and respected, never forgotten.

But what is it hanging in the tokonoma? People often ask, so here is the weird and wonderful tale, woven together from memories as best I can.

When Liga began teaching *ikebana* at the Sogetsu school of traditional flower arranging in central Tokyo in the late 1990s (invited by grand master Hiroshi Teshigahara, an old flame from way back) she was asked to rectify a balance that he feared had become distorted over the years: Nature taking second place to experimentation and profit. Surely it was wrong to cut down a flowering cherry tree in its prime and describe that as flower arranging — something I had always thought and often tried to articulate.

So Liga initiated a class that used natural materials that had been thrown away or outgrown their use . . . dried flowers and branches rather than fresh-cut. Prunings. Cuttings. The only rule was to try not to kill anything deliberately in order to create something else. In this case, Art. A kind of vegetarian ikebana; vegan in its purest form.

Anyway I went to the first exhibition by her students — a truly inspirational eye-opening event — and many were happy to give away pieces rather than lug them home to often far-flung parts of Japan.

In this case, what had arrived as a bundle of green twigs hung with bright red berries pruned from an overly-rampant creeper, was now a piece of woven cosmic sculpture of outstanding beauty and potential. In the exhibition it was standing on its side on the floor, as if inviting some animal, bird, reptile or even a very small child to creep inside and rest.

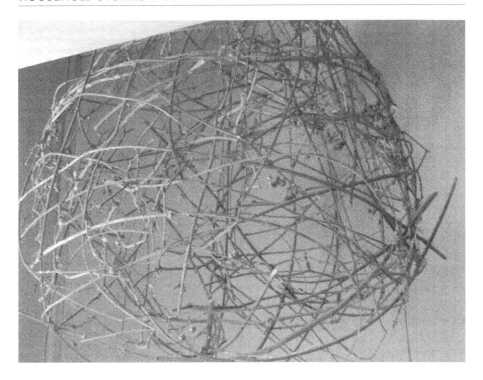

Looking back, I'm not sure how I got it back to Hayama, but I did, and placed it respectfully in my own art alcove. Whereupon Tora went crazy, thinking it something quite wonderful to bat about, jump on and play with. So I hung it up, and it has been hanging ever since, albeit in a different location, now brown and desiccated but still intact and looking remarkably like a giant bird's nest.

Very *marui*, now I come to think about it.

The sloping angled nando in the right-hand corner is under the eaves of the roof, so it's not easy to get in and out, though needs must. It houses the heater in summer, the fan in winter, plus boxes of imported quilts and quilt tops.

"Why?" you might ask.

Most of them are African-American in origin, and how they came to be here rather than in Alabama, and all those other Southern States with a past rooted in slavery is a lesson itself.

Trying to complete a book in 2009, I found myself being tested right, left and centre with regards to focus and willpower.

I remember the day when old programming first began trying to trap me into going backwards rather than forwards — an ad in a magazine reporting auditions for a new production by Tokyo International Players (TIP).

Now I have not acted on stage since the 1960s, having made the decision that if I was not going perform professionally I was not going to perform at all. Yet suddenly I found myself whipping off an e-mail to say I was interested. Catching myself procrastinating, I slapped my wrist and went back to work.

A day or so later I found myself talking with a friend about starting to paint again and went out and bought canvasses, paints and brushes. I even started something, but still it stands unfinished.

And then, surfing eBay while still awaiting inspiration, I found not just quilts — an interest in a former life — but African American quilts, about which I knew nothing and which provided the perfect distracted excuse to determine to know more. I ordered reference books about history, pattern and symbolism, and began buying. . .

Boxes began to arrive, much to Akii's concern. "What, another?" he would mutter in worried fashion, as surreptitiously I tried to whisk them upstairs without being seen.

I had a lot of fun, though . . . a great exhibition at RBR in Tokyo celebrating African-American Month, with a good half dozen sold. Shows and sales here, too, with quilts and tops slung from bamboo poles or over trees and walls. Even a day at the Zushi antique market, where quilts and tops found new homes roundabout.

Quilt tops are the part of the process that quilters love most . . . piecing together even the smallest scraps of precious fabric imaginable to create a pattern and design. Often they would get tucked away, with plans to turn them into proper quilts later, but then forgotten. Many have survived, often as bright and clean as the day they were finished and stored.

Hard to sell? Not really. Responding emotionally to the colour, the vibrancy, people hang or drape them, make them into curtains or throws, or just like to look, touch and admire, marvelling at the creativity and wondering about the financially impoverished but richly creative life of the woman who made it.

Barefoot I move softly, comfortably across the tatami matting to where, directly ahead, and running the full length of the two rooms, are windows that provide a panoramic view (all things being relative) down over Zushi between green hills.

This is slightly let down by the fact that Nonaka-san's house below our own has a flat roof that is slowly and surely peeling off. But no matter: as noted before, this is how one survives in Japan, not necessarily by activism to effect changes for the better, but by psychologically editing out the unpleasant and unwanted and concentrating on what pleases most.

And right now, what pleases most is the wild wisteria clouding the hillsides (those parts that have so far avoided being concreted) with swathes of purple flowers. Three weeks ago the view was blushed pale pink with cherry blossoms. Always changing . . . In autumn, the brilliant hues of maple set the hills on fire; in winter trunks and branches hang in space, stark in black on white, like a *sumi* ink painting.

But all is not perfection. If I slide open a pane, lean out and look to the left, a wall of concrete rises harshly into the sky at the end of our enclave; turn my head right and there is a hideous gash of dirty grey concrete, and then a three-storey building of glass and steel that appears more a goldfish bowl than a home.

Wondering how it got planning permission in what is essentially a residential area boggles the imagination, until you learn the owners have a construction company which they run onsite while living on the two floors above.

Anyway, planning permission is pretty much an alien concept in this country; if you can afford a piece of land you can do just about whatever you want with it, and hang the neighbours.

Leonardo and Shinobu bought a patch further down the hill and designed a house that would accommodate both his two-metre-tall Italian frame and a growing family. But he always said that if ever he could not look out of one particular window and see green, he would leave. Returning in the new year after several months in Italy, studying to be a sommelier, he found the trees gone and a wall being cemented in their place. He's very angry, very depressed.

We are quite high up here. So high that when I hang futon out of our windows to air — as do most self-respecting households each and every morning — they dry in no time at all here, in the warm to brisk sea breezes off the ocean.

Exactly how many metres above sea level I have often wondered but never quite get around to checking. Climate-warming and rising sea levels apart, I no longer trust the sea in quite the way I did before coming to Japan and would never, ever, however wonderful the location or view, choose to live near a beach.

Memories of the tsunami that, while sweeping away tourists and local people alike from Thailand's Patong Beach, ravaged hundreds of miles of Sri Lanka's coastline, and also affected Indonesia, India and the Maldives, are still too raw.

We went with Ken last year to explore a colony of houses built by Americans after the war, overlooking a small cove secreted away near Aburatsubo, down the coast towards Misaki. If someone did not buy them they were to be demolished and the whole area developed and in Japan, we all know what that means: environmental ruination.

Ken had his eye on one house down on the water's edge — he would sit on the kitchen floor, dangle his legs out over the sea and imagine hanging out a rod to catch his supper. Romantic for sure but not for me, preferring to fantasise about the one on the very top of the hill.

He never did get enough people together to buy out the lot in a cooperative effort, but the good thing is that as far as I know, they — and the forest and abundant wildlife all around — are all still there.

For now, at least . . .

As in quiet, relatively natural places anywhere, sleep comes swift and easy. Unless the sky is clear and the moon full, in which case I toss and turn and eventually get up, fetch a stool quietly and go into the other room-space so as not to disturb Akii, to open that window and moon-bathe. I like squinting, half closing my eyes to bring the auras around trees and along skylines into focus, listening to the night owls, and for any passage of wind through the moon-shining night air.

It is a house where sleep is deep and long, for which I am always grateful. Even when typhoons blow through, we have the *amado* to protect us. All the larger windows have these traditional 'storm doors', wooden shutters that can be drawn (from slots built into outside walls) to right and left to cover the glass, and then slid back inside to be near invisible after extreme weather has abated.

Whoever is responsible for the anonymous Irish proverb that speaks of sleep as the beginning of health is worthy of great respect. I follow my body in what it needs in terms of sleep, and mostly it is a lot. Sometimes less, occasionally even more. But I know if I have not had enough — nothing feels right and my joints scream.

Some may consider me a lazy wastrel for believing I need a good eight to nine hours a night, but that is not my problem.

Again I draw attention to a quote, this time by Lord Byron, from his poem "The Dream," *Sleep hath its own world/And a wide realm of wild reality.* It is into this other world that I slip with open arms and an open mind, ready, willing and able to explore and embrace other levels of reality to return refreshed.

We sleep on futon, the cotton floor mattresses now known the world over, with small pillows stuffed with buckwheat *soba* (warm in winter, cool, in summer) and a modern duck-down-filled duvet on top. Akii sleeps on the right, nearest to the tokonoma; I to the left and, if turned away from him, facing the other part of the room, half cut off by sliding *fusuma* doors.

We are not much over-looked, only by two hanging lights that came with the house, and which are balanced in their ugliness by two water colours hung high, one in each room, both bought on early trips abroad. The one we face as we read or sleep is Korean — pink blossom on brown branches of plum; the one in the other room is Chinese, green vine leaves and twining tendrils. Both are very lovely.

Along the wall on the far side, from left to right in this order, is the rattan recliner, complete with a foot-rest, that I bought for my mother when she visited us in Hayama in the spring of 1991. She came to celebrate her eightieth birthday, having never flown before in her life. It was only after she died I realized that she had in large part made such an effort to try and make up for the fact that most of her love and concern had been directed at my sister, who was more obviously needy.

Such revelations often come too late.

The two flat cushions used to pad the seat of the chair and relieve the back are home to two smaller and plumper relations, one in pale gold silk and the other woven from flax and dyed with indigo.

Both came from Afa, an atelier in Hayama that creates wonderful clothes and interior goods from natural — preferably organic — fabrics. Michiyo, who created the label, travels the world working with weavers and dyers to give traditional techniques a conceptual contemporary twist.

I try to buy one or two pieces from her every May, when she opens her studio by the river during Golden Week; her clothes are so timeless and wonderfully easy to wear. (But again, sadly, not this year.)

A large cotton indigo-dyed hanging, now immensely faded, pinned onto the wall alongside the chair shows two stylized feathers laid vertically side by side within a circle.

In Japanese, the word *kamon* refers to a family crest. Just as clans in Scotland wore various tartans to differentiate one warrior in battle from another, so Japanese foot soldiers had motifs printed on flags or clothing, and chieftains wore helmets that often were designed around their family crest.

Akii had told me that his own kamon (*mon* in short) for the Ueda family, consisted of two feathers crossed within a circle. But I misunderstood and bought the hanging as a gift, thinking I had done something really clever.

Wrong.

But he was immensely kind, and very creative in his response: "Never mind. It's better . . . We're together, secure within the circle, but separate."

At the time I was touched and appreciative. It has always been very important to me within any relationship to be left alone. For my psyche and energy to be respected, not encroached or leeched upon, vandalised in any way.

What a joke then to be told only recently that he had got it wrong completely; it was not his mon at all. Nor would he or could he provide any further enlightenment, indicating I guess that the subject is far more interesting to me than it has ever been to him.

I have found this among many Japanese of his generation, born in the post-war period; an amazing ignorance about their own culture, and really not all that bothered. An attitude exemplified by the relaxed attitude towards knocking down historic buildings.

I remember just a year or so ago sitting in the garden of the Nagashima family's two hundred-year-old Edo Period house in Zushi (one of only half a dozen remaining in the town) and Catharine's husband Koichi — she a Welsh-born town planner, he an architect — asking if I knew how many protected buildings there were in the UK.

Sixty thousand, it seems.

"In Japan," he said sadly, "just six thousand and decreasing. If earthquakes and typhoons do not destroy heritage, commercial interests will."

But back to our tatami room . . .

Three zabuton — terracotta, dusky pink and turquoise — stacked, for Akii's rakugo practice.

Then a finely decorative woven and carved wood and bamboo screen, bought in the flea market at the citizens' festival near the Arena sports centre in Zushi some four years ago. Amazingly, it cost less than a thousand yen.

And finally, tucked into the corner, a *tansu*, from the recycle shop that Catherine and I used to frequent before she left for Victoria. Sadly, like just about everything else in the house, it has suffered Tora's clawing and can truly be said to be worth next to nothing.

But still it serves its purpose, accommodating my scarves, Akii's kimono, *obi* sashes and accessories for story-telling, and our bed linen, quite beautifully.

On the top stands a small antique-style lamp in metal and paper. Also Tabei-san's old sewing box, which I really mean to repair some day; one hinge requires tightening and a small piece of wooden edging needs to be glued back into place.

If you remember, she was our landlady in Hayama, living next door, and I never did get my head around the Japanese *keigo* she used on a daily basis, language so old and classically refined, Akii said, that sometimes even he could not understand her.

My mother had admired Tabei-san from a distance with a certain degree of awe, and as a dressmaker herself, very much approved that I had saved something that showed we were so like-minded. It shocked us both that all her belongings could be dumped so ignominiously as rubbish after she died.

Today there is a straw hat on top of the box that has her name

written inside the lid, but this nothing to do with Tabei-san. It is a man's hat, rather like a boater.

Where did it come from?

I remember only that a Japanese woman in a DOTWW workshop wrote about how her grand-father used to wear a hat just like that! She had not thought about him for years, but the picture she sketched in words was of such vivid and unexpected intensity that it made her cry.

Yes, this marvellous multi-functional space is where Akii and his rakugo friends make people roll around with laughter, while I provide people with the tools they need to dig deep with words. But not at the same time . . .

As you know from the introduction on pages i - iii, Drawing on the Writer Within began as drop-in classes at a new creative arts centre in Tokyo named RBR (for Right Brain Research). It was based on Kristin's drawing workshops, but expanded and branched out into many other areas of artistic exploration and endeavour, including writing.

When Kristin asked me what I was going to do at/for RBR, I remember thinking that maybe I could apply right-brain techniques to writing, trick the left-brain (which says, "You can't write/only writers write/don't even try," etc.) into shutting down and taking a back seat so that creativity could be released to run its natural course, and in association, confidence restored.

While beginning with weekly classes in Moto-Azabu, I had also gathered a group from around the neighbourhood here to meet once a month on a Saturday afternoon. But something was not right. The techniques worked fine, but how to handle the emotions that came flowing to the surface as a result? It was through a lot of reading, seeking a solution, that I came to incorporate Proprioceptive Writing into the work, developing seemingly organic courses that naturally led writers onwards and upwards, one into another.

PW — a practice that can quite literally transform lives by helping us explore our thinking on paper — was developed in the 1970s by two university English professors in America, Linda Trichter Metcalf and Toby Simon. Their book, *Writing the Mind Alive – The Proprioceptive Method of Finding Your Authentic Voice*, has proved invaluable over the years.

By incorporating PW into my own programme, Drawing on the Writer Within, students have a means by which to investigate the emotions and reactions that arise during exercises, so allowing me to concentrate on the writing rather than being drawn into the role of therapist.

Level 1 of DOTWW, Initiation, works beautifully in this room (and on tables in the dining room downstairs) as two Sunday workshops. The other courses have to be weekly, and in Tokyo, as there are regular assignments based on work done in each class.

I love to see newcomers leaning against the walls, visualizing, or sprawled on the tatami, writing.

There were two students here just two days ago (a third having failed to make it on the day; she got on the wrong train and woke up miles away, in completely the wrong direction) and their faces were so relaxed and pure in the sunlight:

"Lovely," they would say as a semi-tropical Pacific breeze blew up from the ocean through the screened open windows.

"Ahhhh," they would murmur, smelling the green from the hillsides, wild flowers in profusion.

"Amazing," they would gasp as they heard their thoughts and imaginings in words as never before.

Nice. Very nice. But to be honest, it's all a mystery; I don't know how and even why DOTWW works. But it does. And, once again, I'm so grateful.

Creativity and healing, relaxation and laughter . . .

And as if these are not gifts enough, a room with a view.

THE DRESSING ROOM/STORE ROOM NO. 3

mittsume no nando

We are especially fortunate and grateful to have a space we can call a dressing room. Described as yet another store room, it may have doubled as a bedroom; it was certainly big enough, with windows on two sides, out to the back and towards the Tanaka house just above us but the glass frosted, as if demanding privacy.

Interesting. I had not thought of that before.

The floor, which is laid with a simple parquet of short wooden planks and polished, is less than one-quarter taken up with a wardrobe (Akii's, for his business suits) and has another larger measure occupied by two *tatami*-topped boxes which, when unstacked and laid side by side, create a stage for *rakugo*. (Inside? More quilts.) Cover it with a red cloth, top with a large red *zabuton* and hey presto . . . or in more colloquial British terms, bob's your thespian uncle.

(Actually he — Bob, from Robert — was my father, but that's a much earlier story.)

The other half is occupied by a short red-sprayed rail for my clothes, and white plastic stacking boxes from Muji — four for Akii, four for me. There are four more of these on the shelf that runs along the left-hand wall as you walk in, and above the window opposite.

There is a custom of changing clothes in Japan that may seem odd to many, but makes perfect sense in a country where space is regarded as being at a premium.

On May Day it has always been traditional to shake out summer cottons and silks and store away winter clothes, then on the first day of October to go into reverse — put away summer clothes and bring out warm coats and sweaters for winter.

Right now, drawers are still full of socks and long-sleeved T-shirts, so we are late this year, but that is because temperatures are still fluctuating, sometimes warm, sometimes cold. But we are getting close to relinquishing winter, and about time too. Right now I am so sick and tired of the few clothes I own.

I remember Judi coming to stay in Hayama, years ago now. A former journalist in Manchester, who for years wrote about beautiful homes for interior design magazines, she looked around the house with interest but then asked where on earth I kept my clothes.

There, I said, pointing to a rail.

Yes, she said, but what about the rest of them?

There was no rest of them, I explained. The rail was it. I kept things tight by buying selectively, and if I did not wear something in three years, it was passed on.

Poor Judi. It took a while for this to sink in. It transpired that she had wall-to-wall closets in virtually every room upstairs in her terraced cottage, jam-packed with clothes dating back to when she was a teenager.

My sister was the same, with sixty blouses! (I know because I counted them after she died.)

No, she didn't wear the large majority, Judi supposed, thoughtfully. And went home three weeks later with at least a challenged perspective, if not a new intent.

Having said all this, I do have some items that I hold on to for nostalgic reasons only. But not to the extent of having sixty of anything . . . I'm not sure I have had sixty of anything in my life — oh, barring money, sheets of blank paper, books and music tapes and CDs . . . a matter of my own personal priorities, I am beginning to realize, shame-faced.

Because there is also the bag in my study cupboard with all the letters ever received in Japan, up until e-mail began to take over from snail mail in the late 1990s. These days the only personal letters I receive are from my aunt, now in her early nineties, and even these are typed! (She was a super-duper secretary; she still loves her vintage Olivetti and is mentally alert, with hands and eyes as good as ever.) There are cards on occasion, but sadly letter-writing is an art and craft being fast consigned to the past.

But back to the present, and — reaching up onto the top shelf to rummage through assorted suitcases and backpacks — I pull down a knee-length multi-coloured sweater with ballooning clown-like sleeves, all tied up in a plastic bag.

Immediately I am transported back to 1976, when I helped put together a book of the craziest knitting patterns imaginable: *Wild Knitting.*

It was on that project for the UK publisher Mitchell Beazley (now part of the Octopus Publishing Group) that I met three women now regarded as being among my closest friends: Louise, who long ago emigrated to Australia; Sandy, more recently removed to Somerset; and Debbie, still in London. Also on the editorial team were Linda, Jane, Ingrid and Patsy. Other inspired knitwear designers — Debbie apart — included Val Moon, Sandy Black, Rosie Tucker and Betty Barnden, to name just a few.

But what is this sweater doing here in Japan? I have no memory of bringing it, and why on earth would I do so? Did I really think that I might someday wear it? It would be better off in the Victoria and Albert Museum, and in writing these four words, I find I have made a decision: this is where it will go — or at least be offered — together with a copy of the book.

Wild Knitting is quite famous now for being so bold in its day. As a pioneering K1, P1 classic, sought-after vintage copies now command cultish high prices, or so Amazon.com seems to indicate.

Being long out of print, I would rather it was being reprinted, but then you can't have everything. Knitting, like everything else, has moved on. Especially me.

The only bag or basket that draws my eye is a backpack woven from bamboo. I bought it in Bontoc on that trip by jeepney across the mountains of the northern Philippines, and returned to Japan with it stuffed with weaving and more weaving.

Now the only things inside are a dozen rectangles of old glass delicately painted with flowers, wrapped in pages from a newspaper dated 1988. I removed them from some old broken Chinese lamp many years ago (the details of which and how and where now evade me), and fully intend to do something with them some day . . .

So, joining all these pieces of fabric and bits of china hoarded away, they wait for a rainy day, when inspiration strikes or suddenly I find time on my hands. Ha!

But thinking about bags makes me recall one tucked into a drawer of the *tansu* in the tatami room just described. It is an antique pouch in black velvet embroidered in gilt and silk threads with a peacock.

I keep it because Ena gave it to me — now there is a name I have not dallied with for some time, but we did correspond when I first came out here, until her letters tailed off and I realized I was doing all the work. I was fond of her, but sadly on occasion there comes a time you have to let people go. She was a knitting specialist also, had married late, moved to salubrious suburbia, had a son. He must be in his thirties now.

Inside the silk lining of the clutch bag, in a pocket is a note that reads: "To Angela, Happy Birthday, Love, Ena." How interesting that I am just one week away from my birthday, and her own was also in May, making us both a Gemini.

Since I do not believe in coincidences, ought I to consider it a message? Am I being encouraged to seek her out again, get in touch?

I remember gathering a team for a publishing project in the Seventies and discovering that over half of the women recruited

were Gemini. Was I seeking my twin? Or was it pure narcissism —
gazing into the mirror to find comfort in so many alter egos? We
were all very different — and temperamentally very difficult, I do
remember that.

But, as a creative team? Unbeatable.

It is also pretty unbeatable to have an iron bridge out of the back
window of your dressing room. But that is what we have.

When first constructed, it enabled occupants to cross the gap
between the back of the house and the mountainside and step straight
into green to go walking and hiking. How lovely that must have been.

When the second layer of concrete was added, rising higher
and no longer granting access to Nature, a ledge was created, wide
enough to sun-bathe but not much more. When we first moved in
we used to go out every autumn to cut down the *susuki* grass and
prune shrubs that had taken root through cracks in the concrete.

Now the bridge is as unsafe as the entry to the cave; it's rusting
fast and slowly falling to pieces. Sad to open the window and see
how once it must have been.

Our landlady knows of its sad state, but chooses to do nothing
about it.

If for reasons of her own she is allowing the house to decay
around us, we must be careful not to be here when it finally gives
up the ghost.

MY ROOM
watashi no heya

I don't know why, but just beyond the sliding doors to the *nando*, there is a metre of wall before the entrance to my room, and a step.

The reason and purpose of this step — no more than three centimetres high, if that — eludes. Even Tora forgets on occasion and stumbles, it being quite hard to see the way forward if my door is closed. As for me, my toes are imprinted — nay, dented — with the word "Fuck".

There is a lovely, shallow, flat, woven basket hung on the wall, from the store on Ginza-dori in Zushi that sells all manner of household goods created from bamboo: brooms, rakes, mats, baskets, chopsticks, massage blocks . . .

Just last Sunday, with a workshop in progress, a writer asked what it was.

For sun- and wind-drying fish, I replied . . . you know . . . you see them laid outside in fishing villages. You don't recognise it because it's flat against the wall to reveal the weave on the underside.

"*Naruhodo* (Ah, now I see!)", she said.

And then went away satisfied enough to write about it.

On the door, an Apple logo sticker. Funny how there are Windows people, and Apple people . . .

As a Windows person, Akii finds my Macbook wanting in just about every respect. But let's not go there, because it is one of the few areas in which we end up arguing. I mean, what's wrong with a computer being user-friendly? To him this somehow equates as not being serious: serious professionals use Windows; Apple is for people who like playing . . .

Okay, Angela, stop.

Let's look on the far side of the door for distraction, and what do we find but two posters: one with a head of purple iris (a botanical illustration), the other half a temple in pink and red with black lettering advertising an exhibition of contemporary *hanga* wood prints by 'Naoko', as commissioned to illustrate the Heian-Period compilation of Japanese short stories, *Konjaku Monogatari*.

I love this room. How many thousands — millions — of words have been written in here? How many trillions of thoughts have chased through my endlessly chattering brain? How many breaths have I taken to live through each and every day? How many deliberate slow breaths have I taken trying to enter stillness and silence, or to consciously allow energy to enter my body and heal the various parts that at one time or another scream for attention? (There are really parts of this ageing thing I could well do without.)

I no longer practise yoga, which I had done on and off for many years, and miss it terribly. I dream of being in lion's pose, it is — was — so comfortable.

But I do sit.

And sometimes I dance.

There is music playing now, from Songlines' Top of the World CD 75: in-between tracks from the albums *Beyond the Horizon* (Yo Yo Ma and the Silk Road) and Steve Riley & the Mamou Playboys' *C'est Trop/Too much.*

Designed to get toes tapping, this Cajun offering has me whirling across the floor as if I was born yesterday. Trouble is, I wasn't. So let me slow down gently like a Sufi dervish coming to rest after a whirling meditation, to stand still in the centre of the room and with quiet uncritical eyes take stock.

There are windows on three sides, out onto the back wall across the angled roof over the *genkan*, over the side of the house facing the drive and the Tanaka house up above, and across shrubs and trees to over and beyond Nonaka-san's wilting roof (today puddled with water because it is raining) towards Zushi.

Often in the morning, just as I sit down to begin writing or research, there is a rush of wings outside, and a kite (*tombi*) alights on the top of the leaning pole of Pisa that carries wires and cables to the house, so enabling me to work at home as I do and remain in touch with the outside world.

These birds of prey are common in Japan, and I have always felt privileged to be so close. This magnificent specimen, with a wing span of near some two metres, usually stays for half an hour or so, alternatively watching the ground for waste food or small vermin, and fixing me with a watchful eye that seems to say, So here we are again, you doing what you do, and I doing what I do.

Now (time passing swiftly when at work) it is five o'clock, as marked loudly just now by the community chime — a megaphone system that extends into the most remotely populated valley. Controlled from City Office, it informs young children that it is time to go home, and also instructs we adults on what to do and when in what is essentially a kindergarten society. (Infuriating on a daily basis, a godsend in emergencies.)

In winter the landscape allows me to see Dinky-sized trains running left to Kurihama and right to Tokyo, down below the entrance to our valley. Then there are the rooftops of the town, with some buildings standing higher than others, hindering a clear view to the coast.

I cannot claim to see water, but as I look down towards the Pacific (next stop California) — and if the weather is kind — I am sometimes allowed to see a small snippety smudge of purple shadow that is the Izu Peninsula, and the light changing off the ocean, both quite good enough.

I love to sit and watch the sky, the chasing clouds, the passage of the sun from left to right, the changing passions of the moon, the near-invisible backward drift of precessing stars, the ever-changing inconstant illumination of sky-scape and heavens.

Yes, I love the universal sweeping embrace of this room . . .

Apart from the ceiling (polystyrene tiles that I ignore), all the walls and cupboards are lined and faced with wood, turned warmly dark with time and sun.

The parquet flooring — wooden blocks laid in a pattern — consists of alternate squares of plain and marquetry (six narrow widths each, some dark, some light) laid in different directions for a puzzle effect. I use them often as a point of focus in meditation, gazing down rather than up.

As for furnishings and decoration, they seem to spiral out from the centre, so this is where I will start, standing under the central lampshade — based on Isamu Noguchi's famed circular design with a criss-crossing frame of bamboo covered with a deliberately uneven handmade paper that looks like a constellation of stars when switched on.

Akii has one in his room also.

A clutch of Christmas cards hang from the pull, all made by Buffy but over a number of years, so with Ross and white boxer Axel in 2003, then grandson Max born in April 2006 (Axel died soon after Max was born, as if making way for the baby he had been substituting for), and Max wearing a Santa hat in 2009.

Why these three made it, and not the others, I have no idea. But they are my earthquake monitor; I can roughly judge the strength of a tremor by their motion, the violence of the swing. Sometimes when smaller inconsequential tremors are regular, I'm enabled to type in tune.

Moving clockwise, I am on a rug, woven in an Inca design in black, grey and terracotta on beige, and carried back from Mexico.

Azzah took us to a friend's gallery, and both Akii and I chose one for our workrooms. His folded sensibly into his backpack. My own, being large and heavy, I had to hoist onto my shoulder.

Trust me to give myself such a hard time. Would I put myself through such trouble now? Maybe, but hopefully not.

There is a light woven rag rug under the desk in navy, grey, brown and lemon, but disintegrating; Akii has one too, in brighter colours. I have no memory of where they came from, but not as far as Mexico!

Facing the back window, I try not to think in too much detail about the contents of the cupboards top and bottom.

Those above, which have outwards opening double doors, contain boxes of negatives (from the days of film), bags of letters. There is also a mass of reference material for a book I once thought to write — a 'her-story' of Japan . . . this country as told through women's contributions to society over the millennia.

The idea came after reading every 'his-story' book I could lay my hands on when I first came here, and realising that I was lucky to find more than two or three women mentioned in any of them, and then always the same names.

I wrote to every prefecture asking for information on all the famous women they laid claim to. Nearly every one replied. But then I realized the enormity of the job I was about to take on, and I was only passing through, not staying here, right? So I put it aside. A pity as by now it would have long been finished.

Yes, of course there is a lesson here too, but the dust continues to gather.

The cupboards below with sliding doors go under the eaves of the roof, but there are shelves, mostly taken up with files of clippings of articles and profiles from *The Japan Times*, for whom I wrote for near on twenty-five years.

There are many interviews I feel proud of from the thirteen hundred or so conducted over the decades, not because of my words but rather from the privilege of meeting so many extraordinary people.

It still amazes me that on first meeting strangers could be so trusting, and I can honestly say — apart from one abortive early piece, when I was so anxious to impress that I crossed a line and lost a potential friend — that when anyone said "Off the record", that is how it remained.

There are also cartons of old Christmas and birthday cards, and what I call my treasure box. This is where I hoard special handmade greetings and gifts, many from so long ago I have forgotten their origin and who gave me them. A good sort out is required. Followed by a ritual burning.

(In the Dark Ages, I would have been burned as a witch for such a thought, which I hold in mind . . .)

An easel stands in front, slightly to the right towards the bookcase. The canvas on it has been there for three years, unfinished, from that time I thought I'd start painting again. I did, but then stopped. It was not that I became depressed but rather quite like it as is — taken from a photograph of Buffy and her original white boxer, Nellie — a work in progress.

But maybe I am just making excuses . . . I know how I want to finish it, with the words she had written on the back of the pic, but curling around the painted images: *Isn't it funny how people end up resembling their pets????*

I can see the line now, in the fine italic I learned at school, but how to get to the point where I can start to finish? So many times I look at it. Walk around it. Walk past it. Address it . . . sometimes affectionately, sometimes in self-hectoring tones. Even sit down and pick a brush out of the Chinese vase that sits on the shelf below the work not in progress.

But that's as far as it gets.

The black bookshelf that sits neatly into the corner is one

of a pair; the other is diagonally across the room against the fourth wall.

On top are two recorders — descant and baroque — as learned to play in primary school and that I still do, walking about, picking out tunes; and a vintage projector Made in Japan (the Birdie model by the Fuji Photo Film Co., Ltd), picked up in a flea market.

Also an equally vintage typewriter used by a Japanese journalist who wrote well into her nineties, but whose name and story is now faded from memory and she, sadly, long passed on; a boxed plastic kit by Tamiya for making the 148 Nakajima K1841A Hayate (Frank) fighter plane (Akii's friend Naito-san's father flew one during the war); and rolls of posters accumulated over the years . . . They include a striking full-length black and white fashion photograph of Nik in his Bubble Years of balletic/modelling prime, and one day it will be framed and hung as deserved.

One day . . .

As for the books, they are out of control. Every few months I cull, and nowadays few are novels. There's a lot of poetry, I realize, but mostly the titles are non-fiction and concerned with change and transformation or prehistory.

There are some biographies, autobiographies, and books concerning travel, serious and humorous.

Plus all my reference books for *Chasing Shooting Stars*, which focused on a trip made to Argentina, Chile and Uruguay in search of family roots and answers. Needless to say, I got more than I bargained for, so providing the kick start I needed to start a far more important journey — what Swami Radhanath calls in his book of the same name, "the journey within".

Lots of music too, packing some of the smaller shelves and — turning the corner — spreading along the top of the *tansu* on the second wall. (I am still travelling clockwise . . .)

A fine length of Japanese rag weaving — much faded, most

likely incredibly grubby — runs over the surface from left to right, hanging down each side, and piles of CDs — classical, baroque (for workshops) and individual albums and compilations of world music, these last courtesy of *Songlines*, the bi-monthly magazine concerning world music, published in Oxford, England, that falls into my mailbox as regular as clockwork.

Right now though, *Cenc Sufi* is playing on the Sanyo system Akii bought me for Christmas one year; nice sound. The music, described as Mystical Acoustic, and by Osman Murat Tugsuz, not only covers guitar and keyboard sounds but combines them with traditional Turkish instruments such as oud (*ud*), zither (*kanun*) and the reed flute known as *ney*.

It brings back memories of meeting Akii in Istanbul for Christmas in 2009 (I flying from Scotland, where I was staying three months to be close to my aunt, he from Japan) and seeing Sufi monks meditating in circular motion towards what in Zen Buddhism is called *satori* (enlightenment).

But wait — I have forgotten the two pictures hanging between the tansu and the bookcase.

One is a pencil sketch drawn by my mother of herself playing her cello. It is simple yet bold, with great energy. It would have been done after art school sometime in the 1930s, when she was at Sunfield, the first pioneering Rudolf Steiner residential home in the UK, located in Clent, just outside Birmingham.

She worked there for six years, met my father there, and married there; near enough a year later, I was born there. She played in quartets and also with the Birmingham Symphony Orchestra in those days; now I have her cello in Scotland, and in January bought a teach-yourself-how-to-play textbook to take back on my next trip. Another New Year resolution . . .

Want to take bets?

The other picture always stirs interest, especially among

student writers. For it shows a young Japanese girl in a red dress, her dark hair piled high, kneeling on a *zabuton* and writing on a low circular table, just like the one I have in the big *tatami* room next door and used in workshops. Dated 1935-10-6, the painting is signed simply, Hiroko.

No more is known.

To add to the mystery, I found it among a pile of papers in a junk shop somewhere in Tokyo, and when I asked the owner how much, his eyebrows shot up into his wig. It's torn, he noted . . . and indeed the top half and left-hand sides do look as if they have been nibbled by mice. But when I insisted, he shrugged and suggested 500 yen.

A better deal I have never made in my life. It's truly lovely, and because of the stillness of her pose and focus, very inspiring. Because of these qualities it is one of the items Akii says he would grab from this room if there ever is a fire. (Hopefully, I am also on his list!)

The only other item of significance on top of the tansu is my small light box and a magnifying glass for checking out slides. Redundant, I suppose, in current digital days, but I have many boxes of slides and like to check them out from time to time.

These boxes spill into the cabinet below, while the three drawers underneath contain stationery both used and new, and all the original materials relevant to CSS: the letters from my grandfather in Buenos Aires to my father in Coventry (1936–1954); photos; masses of memorabilia.

And in thinking about Sam (Samuel Edward Charles Loader) I feel a frisson of guilt that I have done nothing about his remains in the British Cemetery in Montevideo, the city in Uruguay where he was born in 1881.

I was told ten years ago that if payment was not made on the plot (abandoned after the funeral) and no arrangements were made, his bones would be dug up and incinerated and the land re-used. Then Argentina's economic collapse had a knock-on effect in the region, and all went quiet.

Part of me thinks bones are bones; let them go. But then I think of Sam, and my father, and wonder what they would want me to do. It's an ongoing inner struggle, one that I could well do without.

The window is framed with plain cream cotton curtains from Muji, as are those in the tatami and guest rooms. Drawing those nearest helps shade the small black desk that stands alongside my computer table.

Right now it's a bit messy, with my Filofax, camera (downloading photos), a dictionary, notebook and pen, working notes on scraps of paper, a CD pack for learning Spanish (another ha!) and a small pile of books: *Art of the Personal Essay* (an anthology from the classical era to the present, selected by Philip Lopate); *Hamlet's Mill* (an essay investigating the origins of human knowledge and its transmission through myth, by Giorgo de Santillana and Hertha von Dechend); and the *Writers and Artists Year Book 2010*, well-thumbed in trying to find a home for CSS last year.

Underneath on the single small shelf are stacks of back-up discs for manuscripts and computer manuals.

Forget the restrictive and ancient heating/air-con unit that is fitted into part of the window, and move on to the fact that Tora has just leapt from the roof over the *genkan* below, up and through the part of the window that does open.

(This is called focusing on the positive.)

She jumps down from the ledge to pass sedately under my swivel office chair and my computer to where she can collapse onto the rug for yet another nap.

I have an iMac on the lower ledge of the computer table, which I disconnect to go traveling. Normally it is wired up to a large screen and separate keyboard at chest level, with a small camera perched on top for Skyping (thanks to Susannah for this; she left it here two years ago, en route to scuba diving in Malaysia), and a landline phone to the right.

Several small objects sit along the base of the screen, which I handle every morning before beginning work, or when I get blocked: a black ammonite, given to me by Azzah before she once again left Japan; a pebble painted with a raven (a birthday gift from my aunt Jo years ago), a small piece of fallen debris from the facing of Mexico's Temple of the Sun in Teotihuacán (red clay on both sides with some kind of stone-coloured infilling speckled with mica), plus a small dark stone shaped like a heart and two shells, all from Julia.

We human beings need our occasional rituals and ritual objects and, bereft of the company of my children (and Boots, M&S, and cans of Heinz baked beans) I find comfort in those I have created here.

In the corner to my left, a small black metal shelving unit holds a camera case, and a stack of publications in which I have something in print. On the top, a fax machine, and a carved figure from Africa, rough-hewn from wood. Above hangs another pencil sketch, but this time by friend Catherine of her husband, the poet Erich Fried, who died in Vienna soon after this drawing was done.

She and Erich and their children, twin boys and a girl of Buffy's age, Petra, lived on Exeter Road NW2, but towards the Willesden end rather than in Kilburn. Buffy met Petra (and I, Catherine) on the first day of the girls' starting primary school together with Leah, and her mother Deirdre; they, and we, have been friends ever since.

That time in the early 1970s was extraordinary in so many ways, but especially for knowing Catherine and Erich. Not only was she immeasurably talented as a painter and musician, but Erich was the only poet in the German language capable of filling football stadiums to hear him read, and who had translated some two-thirds of Shakespeare's plays, which are today used as textbooks in German schools.

As a former freedom fighter, who in his youth helped many Jews escape abroad, and (while Jewish himself) a fierce opponent of the Zionist State of Israel, it was commonplace for him to lift the phone and hear the click-clickings of listeners in. He was under surveillance not only by British authorities, but also by the Jewish Right.

One day I arrived to find a former wife ensconced in a spare bedroom; Catherine nursed Nan until she died. She was equally accommodating of Erich's admirers and lovers, who would sit around hanging on his every word.

Another time I was introduced to — and rather fell for — a handsome but haunted-looking man drinking coffee at the kitchen table: the alleged terrorist Rudy Dutschke (leader of the student movement in Germany in 1968), on the run and camping in the back garden.

After Erich died, a museum in Vienna bought his study lock-stock-and-barrel; as the caretaker of his estate, Catherine had to list every book, every scrap of paper, every scribble . . . but at least it kept her occupied, in those empty days following on.

Eventually, with the front room empty — through the windows of which we had all grown used to seeing Erich's massive shaggy head bent low over his desk — she realized it was time to move on. So she did, and now resides in relative calm in Tufnell Park, with Petra and her family — partner Jonathan, and their son Theo — just around the corner.

I do not want to romanticise those days, for there was much I found difficult to process (Catherine appearing to give up so much of herself to be the proverbial doormat to a genius, which involved the stresses and strains — and pain — of living in an open marriage) but they did preoccupy nearly a quarter of my life; their importance cannot be minimalized or trivialised.

I miss settling down with Catherine to read *The Guardian* (always *The Guardian*) and talk as the girls disappeared to play somewhere, and hearing Erich start to shuffle down the corridor at the sound of our voices. Ah Angela . . . he would begin, hewing a slice off the loaf on the breadboard, before starting to question me on this and that.

It took me a long time to stop being intimidated by his academic turn of mind, his acute intelligence, his fame and courage; by then it was too late.

As noted before, I remember him once likening me in public — and in those days there were always so many people going to and fro: German students, friends (locals like Jill and Stuart Hood, and visitors from the US, Russia, all over), family (Nan's son Hans, and Kathy and David from a second marriage, the twins Tom and Klaus and their own buddies, Cat's numerous relatives, innumerable hangers-on) — to an old-fashioned rocking horse.

I'm still trying to work that one out.

On the wall incorporating the town view below, a whiteboard (with the affirmations "Nothing Great is Easy" and "Expectations not Dreams") to try and keep me organized and in balance, with a calendar hanging below.

I used to receive an annual beauty every year from Japan Airlines, thanks to Geoffrey, who was their British agent in International Public Relations for many years. But then he retired and I was dropped from the list; new brooms always sweep clean. Soon after which the airline itself collapsed.

Now I rely on NHK for my annual calendar, and if I ever leave, which I really need to do at some point soon to avoid being the last hanger-on at the party, lord only knows what I will do!

The narrow ledge beneath the window is home to my modem, and from it hangs a crazy tangle of cables and wires, a recycled glass object from Merry — shot with yellow and sparks of gold so always sunny — and two empty boxes. I mean really, what are they for? Nothing, so in to the waste basket they go.

(You would be amazed at how good this exercise has been towards de-cluttering. I just sorted out three piles of *meishi* business cards, for example, reducing them by three-quarters. Now that is progress.)

On the wall above, a framed pastel drawing of a nude, in earth colours on buff paper, from Buffy's days as an art student at George Brown in Toronto.

While below, pinned into the panelling, a black-and-white

postcard of Bruno Groening, the German faith healer and charismatic who was forbidden to practise by Authority (thousands would crowd below his window in the village where he lived) and as a result died soon after in 1957.

You can see in the photograph that his thyroid was massively swollen. It is as if he literally exploded from the build-up of energy in his body that had nowhere to go.

I once attended a meeting where the movement's leader addressed her audience, consisting mainly of Japanese and German devotees, in a style that was more akin to hectoring than lecturing. Quietly writing notes towards the back of the room — I was there in a journalistic as well as personal capacity — I was pointedly admonished and told to either put away my notebook or leave.

I left. Nor did I ever go back.

But I do listen to a tape of Groening's teachings, and I do sit. Sit with my feet flat on the floor and my palms upturned. We are like radio receivers, he advised, believing that health (and healing from illness) is brought about by absorption of the divine life force — in German, the "heilstrom".

I sit here often, on a small stool. I also practise on the train into the city, placing hot energized palms on painful knees for comfort.

One other thing, I have just realized that Buffy's nude is turned away from us, as if unable or unwilling to face the world. We have only a back view, the curve of her back and limbs and ample bum. By contrast, Groening gazes directly into each and every moment, with kind but penetrating eyes that follow me around the room.

There is balance here also.

Between the right-hand curtain and the second black bookcase hang three objects, in a vertical line. Topmost, a painted porcelain plate with a chipped edge (which is why I suppose it was thrown away) as found on our local *gomi* rubbish collection day in Hayama,

and providing a second kick up the backside — synchronistic exhortation — to get on with writing CSS and stop prevaricating. It shows the cruise ship Argentine Maru/Brazil Maru of the Japanese OSK shipping line and is dated 1939.

Below this is a framed photo of a painting Kara did of George — the anarchic Scottish playwright George Byatt — before he died in 1996. I remember having lunch with him in Paris in the summer of '81 and being introduced to the film director Joseph Losey, who was himself enjoying a meal with the writer Francoise Sagan (of *Bonjour Tristesse* fame).

Such a thrill.

A weekend never to be forgotten, both for its happiness and ultimate let-down.

And beneath this bitter-sweet memory, two pressed four-leaved clovers, found on a walk in Hayama in the same clump on the same day. Luck be my lady tonight . . .

Though of course I do not believe in luck, and if such a thing does exist, we create it for ourselves in large part by means of the choices we make. A belief that is exemplified on the second bookshelf (the other's twin) by all the books on Japan that have helped me create my life here, and the many titles on writing, that help towards the creation of Drawing on the Writer Within. Plus innumerable catalogues of exhibitions visited, and files of name cards.

Again, a sort out is required.

On the bottom shelves are all the copies of *Granta* that helped me maintain my equilibrium through the early years, allowing me to keep one literary foot solidly planted in the West, while the other was taking root here. Maybe it would be revealing to sort them into chronological order, to work out when I stopped my subscription. Shall I do that now, or move on?

Move on . . . I'm on a roll here . . .

Rolling forward a foot or so on my designer chair — aluminium frame, with black rubber fittings and red springs — towards my black desk, set at an angle so that I can see the doorway, windows and all corners of the room, except that into which I am more or less tucked. Good feng shui.

This desk, it has to be said, is nothing to write home about, being cheap, contemporary, plastic-coated and melted in various places from candle grease.

(I do Proprioceptive "writes" here in candlelight on a regular basis.)

Drawers down the right-hand side are a jumble of staple guns, paper clips, stamps torn from used envelopes (that's the top one); notebooks and invoice books (middle); and airmail writing pads, envelopes and tape for securing parcels (bottom). On the top surface, an angled Muji lamp, and a small bookcase made by Akii's younger brother Yasumasa, who died in 1978; Akii has one too. My own is fit to bursting with dictionaries and reference books, a pile of plastic files, pencil box containing eagle feathers, scissors, fans, pens and innumerable pencils that could all do with sharpening.

(Note: Buy a new pencil sharpener!)

Two small photos in silver frames: one of Akii in colour, shot on the motorboat crossing to the island on Lake Muskoka, three hours north of Toronto, when Gloria, Ross's mother, still had the cottage; the other a small post-war black-and-white of myself (aged about ten) with my father, mother and sister in the doorway of a holiday caravan in Brixham, Devon.

A pile of books relating to my internal journey: my notebooks covering the years 2000–2010 (workshops, readings, thoughts), a copy of the *I Ching*, and *A Year With Rumi, Daily Readings* (translation by Coleman Barks).

Also files with print-outs, various materials for articles, and on the very top, the face of the Dalai Lama smiling from the front of a file containing correspondence relating to the cottage in Scotland, so he travels even more than he knows.

Sonia and I went to hear this uniquely evolved human being speak at the Pacifico Conference Centre in Yokohama a few years ago. It was a convention organized by a federation of Buddhist sects in Japan, allowing us to gaze down to this tiny beaming charismatic figure seated on the stage over a sea of shining shaved heads.

Alongside the bookcase is a black metal shelving unit, matching the smaller version by the computer table. On the top shelf, a large pink acrylic star, found on Chigasaki beach within days of arrival . . . A sign, I thought.

Plus four small figures, created for TV news programmes but well past their For Sale date, so rescued from a waste bin at NHK: British Prime Minister John Major, US President Bill CLinton, Russian President Mikhail Gorbachev, and Japan's Prime Minister, Tomiichi Murayama.

Below, files of printed and faxed correspondence copies from pre-computer days. When I tell anyone under twenty that when I first came to Japan I was using a typewriter and carbon papers, they look at me as if I am from another planet.

The second holds files of copies of *Asia Magazine*, that I contributed to as their Japan stringer from 1989–1996. How I came to this job at a time when there was a scandalous amount of money flying around (near most of the magazine's funding coming from Japanese advertising) is perhaps another example of how to create your own good fortune.

Travelling in Malaysia, to once again renew my visa, I had booked into a resort hotel up the coast from Malacca to recover from waking one morning in a flop house to find my bed marooned in a sea of monsoon flood water and sewage.

When a colour supplement fell out of the service copy of my room's daily newspaper, I immediately turned to see who was publishing it, and where: Hong Kong, as it transpired, by the China Morning Post Group.

Reading down the list of contributors, I noted that the only country not represented was Japan, which considering that almost all the advertising was Japanese, seemed more than a little odd.

Was there a reason? I faxed the editor from Chigasaki on my return.

(It was a good day; I was feeling strong and confident and even a little cheeky, which I can assure you often fails to be the case.)

The only reason, John the editor replied immediately, was because the Japan stringer had just quit, and was moving on to *The Independent* in London. Did I know him?

Know him? I replied; he (Peter) lives just down the road, in Kamakura.

Which is basically how I got the job. And a very fine job it was too, lasting seven years.

Below is another shelf of files, this time for copies of *TGA EYE*, a client magazine developed for Tokyo General Agency in Tokyo. This company of Japanese women was looking after foreign corporate employees and families when they came to Tokyo, and the president asked me to help after I had written about TGA in *The Japan Times*.

Sadly, my exit was less illustrious.

I had introduced a friend newly arrived from London, who happened to be a very good graphic designer, and *TGA EYE* needed a radical overhaul. Six months later, sick to the teeth with what he perceived of as ridiculous rules and pointlessly endless meetings, and unaware of the consequences according to Japanese custom, he got up from his desk one day and walked out.

Within weeks I was let go.

As I have mentioned before, in Japan, you take responsibility for the actions of others; I got the blame, not he.

But still I regard that time with Tanaka-san and Emi, Shiho and Yumi (the three members of staff I am still in contact with, now all married with families) and the many others as such a privilege; I got to write freely, without interference or censorship, which is rare in the world today.

TGA also supplied me with one of the very first domestic fax machines in Japan — magic enough. Another lucky recipient was ex-pat Susan and her corporate husband, who had a huge house in Kamakura.

Visiting one day, I asked to see their storehouse, which I knew, as Mormons — members of the Church of Jesus Christ of the Latter-day Saints — they would be keeping well in order. What an eye opener that was: toilet rolls for a year, flour and sugar for a year; every household need imaginable for twelve months in preparation for the Apocalypse.

Oh, and I wonder what happened to Karen? She worked at TGA

awhile and then went back to the US and re-invented herself as a security expert. Last heard of she was personal bodyguard to Hillary Clinton, but that was quite a while ago.

The next shelf is a mess. But then order is restored for the lowest of all, where files of original copy from pre-computer days are stored. It was a shock to find these . . . not that they have not been staring me in the face for years, but I had not bent so low for years . . . not since the day I nearly killed myself.

It was in January 2008, when my nerves were still jangled after losing my mother and sister in close succession, but I was trying to pretend that all was well.

Engaged in one of my juggling acts, as in trying to keep any number of work-related balls of activity in the air at one time, I turned, slipped and went flying, first hitting the edge of the desk at floor level and then the corner metal shelving unit. When I stood up, I could not see for blood cascading down my face.

How did I find my way to the toilet and grab a towel to hold to my head while making my way down the stairs, and so down the drive towards Sonia and Yuta? Apparently I was calling for Buffy when they came out to find me.

Treatment: two stitches required to a dissected eyebrow; ten to the laceration on my scalp. I do try to be more careful now; I have acknowledged that I was being told to slow down, and only the harshest wake-up call would apparently do the job.

I wonder if my DNA still adheres to the desk, the shelving . . . how long does DNA last? Something else I am curious to find out.

The pin board is always a riot. Pin boards are, aren't they?

That is their purpose, to be at the receiving end of this and that and the other — postcards of pebbles, bluebells, Cosmati pavements, labyrinths, sacred Sanskrit letters, badges, cartoons, sketches (one by Akii saying I love you in *katakana*; he's holding a bunch of flowers), tickets and receipts. And hiding under it all, a five-pound note that

Michael gave me to put in his Japanese bank account to keep it open, and which obviously I completely forgot.

Sorry, Michael.

Next, a small map of the World Turned Upside Down followed by a regular large-scale Map of the World (a Peters Projection, courtesy of the *New Internationalist*).

With a small painting hung under the upside-down version — a bandoneón player purchased from street-artist Celeste in La Boca, Buenos Aires; and a larger one high up the wall, of me, painted by a girl at a small community art class run by Hiroki at the Moriyama-jinja shrine in Hayama.

Hiroki asked me to model and I was happy to oblige, especially when the young artist (now in her late twenties and possibly with a family of her own, or maybe a pioneer in some creative or academic field) gave me the result. I had spiky blonde hair in those days, and — surprise, surprise — was wearing black, with silver studs in my ears.

Below all this busy-ness stand two, low, wooden filing cabinets, full of paperwork relating to here and the UK.

On the top stands a light. A round, white, glass globe atop a shaped, black, metal pillar in Japanese Art Deco style wearing a hat — a black pillbox with a slice of crimson lace and a black veil.

A hat made by Alan — one of his early samples before he and Barry began their millinery business, and moved from England to Wales, and then to Canada, where they are settled in British Columbia. Buffy modelled it when she was eighteen or so; I sent her the slides, discovered some years ago.

And then there is the attaché case.

The small leather case that launched the adventure into the roots of my ancestral past and took me to South America, and from where it arrived from Buenos Aires in 1954 by ship and rail, containing my grandfather's effects after his death in the Uruguayan seaside resort of Piriapolis.

Looking at it now, the two latches look like eyebrows raised in surprise to find themselves in Japan, the keyholes resemble eyes, the handle a mouth. Ah, now I see — Sam is smiling at me. What a relief. Yet still I don't know what to do about his bones; they haunt me.

I close the door, at the end of my spiralling course around the room, though a figure more representative of the logarithmic Fibonacci spiral — the golden mean, the building block of beauty — than the regular spiral more commonly known ... pull out the chair alongside the last of the filing cabinets, and sit down to face the photograph that the open door keeps hidden from view.

A ghost story, for sure. But with a positive twist, which makes it more or less the perfect exit.

In 2008, I was facilitating a writing course at RBR's new (old) premises in Roppongi. I rarely stayed overnight in Tokyo in those days, so it seemed quite the adventure. I had a sleeping bag, and after waving off all the writers at just after 10 pm, created a nest in the corner of the ground floor (called the first floor in Japan) studio.

An exhibition of photographs had just gone up on the walls —

matsuri (festivals) — but I was too tired to take close note. Instead I climbed into the bag atop a pile of yoga mats, feeling uncommonly smug in the knowledge that I could sleep anywhere, anyhow.

HA! or "*ara*," as they say here.

It was not hard to relax. I was tired — really tired. But surprisingly sleep would not come, and I tossed and turned, turned and tossed, wishing away many of the things unconsidered that had sprung to my lips during class, and turning over all the things I could have more usefully said.

It was at that point I began to hear the voices. Nothing distinct, only the sound of whispering, then a soft tidal chattering and laughing, like waves breaking on the shoreline.

Where was it coming from?

As I turned over towards the doorway, I saw a mist, initially still but then moving, swirling. At the same time I heard the front door open and close and indistinct voices rising and falling, muttering and softening, wreathing and breaking . . .

Initially, I was bemused, then irritated. It was kind of them (whoever they were) not to come in, come closer, but could they not see — understand — how tired I was, that I was trying to sleep? It was so thoughtless and inconsiderate, I mean, really . . .

I tossed and turned back and forth all over again, but this time willing them to be quiet, but then eventually lost my temper and began to weep with fury, opening my mouth to shout, "SHUT UP! GO AWAY! I HAVE TO SLEEP!" But strangely no words emerged, they were stuck in my throat; I was voiceless. Or was I?

It was at this point I wondered if I was dreaming. I have become remarkably adept over the years at waking myself from nightmares. So I woke up, sat up, and there was only moonlight and an extraordinary shining silence and peace throughout the house.

Had I dreamed the whole thing? Had I in fact been shouting in my sleep? How could that have been when my memory now is as clear as at that time? I was there, it did happen, and yet . . . Which was real, then or now? Or was I simply slipping along in two parallel time frames?

It is said that the whole of Minato Ward was once covered with graveyards, which is why RBR asked Christine to clear the house before staff moved in. She, visiting from Australia, had found a samurai warrior lurking in a closet upstairs, and identified a few other souls wandering in limbo, but thought she had persuaded them all to move on.

I believe her.

My phantasmagorical beings were most definitely from a different world, a different time. From my imagination, some might say. Yet what is imagination? Where does it come from and what is it based upon? Maybe the sum of our past life experience; maybe we are simply remembering, on a subconscious level, the innumerable lives we have lived before.

Why are some people more imaginative than others? They aren't.

Maybe — and I say maybe because of course we don't know (except on the gut level of pure intuition) — they are simply more awake, and in this improved state of consciousness, more receptive and open to memory. Or could it be that some souls have more memories than others, simply because they have been around for longer resolving their karma, taking their time to evolve?

When I woke the next morning, the house was full of sunshine, and I saw that I had been lying beneath a monochrome photograph of men carrying a portable Shinto shrine (*mikoshi*) photographed through a spray of light-splashed water — spectators throwing buckets of water to help them cool down.

The title: Purification.

When I got home I rang the photographer, and asked to buy it. Vin was very happy. Vincent . . . Vincent who? I can't read his signature.

Oh lord, now I have to find his meishi, his business card.

I do hope it's not among all those I threw away.

THE GARDEN

niwa

Go ahead or follow me, out of my study (but not forgetting that tricky low step). Along the corridor and in front of the door to the star toilet turn right, then right again down the rest of the stairs.

But wait. Just before, there is a recess on the right, opposite the *tatami* room and between the *nando* and the staircase, containing a built-in sink above a cupboard. Made of copper, this deep sink is reminiscent of those found in *minshuku*, the Japanese equivalent of a B&B or bed and breakfast establishment. Akii and I have stayed in many on our travels, and so often made use of such a washing facility, usually to be found on the corridor outside bedrooms.

When we moved in, a round mirror with long silk tassels hung from the back wall. But I was worried it might get damaged, so I wrapped it up, secreted it away. Instead, we have a carved wooden and painted mirror from Indonesia; the palm trees and parrots are totally out of Japan's traditional comfort zone, of course, but so cheerful!

Okay, now we can turn right down the stairs. And again right at the bottom, past the broom cupboard and into the dining room, sharp right again into the kitchen, and diagonally across to step down to the back door into the garden.

Still with me?

Good.

We are in the space between the back of the house and the mountain wall that rears upwards to trees and sky. It is early June, so the concrete is covered with fresh green Virginia creeper, and flowering honeysuckle hangs down from the overgrown fenced terrace above.

To the right, the bridge rests high above in rusted suspension.

Instead we will head left, to where the wall on the left encloses the *ofuro's* garden. First there is a small door for entering from outside to keep it tidy, then just around the corner I can just see bamboo (*take*, pronounced, in the same way as sake) peeping over the top from inside.

It is at this point the path opens onto a concreted area, with a large, blue, glazed planter overflowing with yellow and orange nasturtiums, and then the window to the guest room to the left, and a hanging basket of flowering cacti.

The *amado* here, fixed to the outer wall on each side of the window, are flaked and peeling; Jeff says he will renovate them (they are all in a similar state) next time he stays, just as he repainted the bench for us last year. A lovely job of it he did too.

Not so lovely are the horizontal lengths of metal piping for drying washing, supported on iron brackets on poles set in concrete blocks. We used to employ lengths of bamboo, which were much prettier and more ecological, but when Glen and Michael left Akiya, we had no more access to *take* growing in situ.

Once cut, bamboo stems, however thick, do dry and weaken to the point of eventual natural decay and collapse, so after two trips to replenish, we had to admit defeat — chrome rods took over. At least they wipe clean; in the old days towels and sheets were often marked on wet days with environmentally friendly but somewhat mucky-looking stripes of natural dye.

Looking to the right, there is a view of houses down below and the hillsides beyond. The descent beyond the wall always was steep; now it is simply a flat blank wall of concrete. The scene (without looking directly down) could be deemed quite attractive, except we remember what it looked like before the trees were all hacked down.

We were hemmed in one hundred per cent by overhanging green, and very lovely it was too. It was a terrible day when the workmen sharpened their axes for the final acts of destruction. With the day already dark and overcast, I lit incense on the table and sat and prayed and chanted. Soon rain began to fall. My chanting grew louder and more desperate as the desecration began. Then thunder rolled across from the sea and lightning began to zigzag across the sky.

The men, who had begun to mutter among themselves, took one last look at this foreign madwoman summoning up powers beyond all our control, and took to their heels, or rather their slippery rain-sodden ropes to reach the relative safety of terra firma below.

Not that it changed anything; the deed was done. Except that last year all the stumps sent up sprouts, and this year both concrete and fencing are beginning to disappear as Mother Nature fights back with reinvigorated wisteria and anarchic swathes of *kuzu* (kudzu) vine in creeping wildness.

Below the slanted ever-lowering wall on this side, topped with pots of shrubs and perennials in flowering profusion, is a short border. Having said this, it's amazing how much is crammed in — three types of mint, parsley, lemon geranium, basil, fennel, a marvellous stand of lemongrass and — planted last year with a kiss and yet more prayers — another of ginger.

The scent of ginger flowers is as distinct and lovely as that from the jasmine that winds along the fencing from this point, so we are looking forward to a veritable potpourri of perfumes this summer.

The small triangular corner plot is planted with trees — plum, persimmon, bay and hydrangeas, lilies, and in spring, hyacinths and freesias. There is a compost heap against the fence, on top of which all vegetable waste is tipped, including eggshells but only after washing, because the membranes inside encourage maggots. (I know they are good for compost, but I'm not good with them after a childhood experience.)

All this helps explain why weeds grow apace and by late July it is impossible to push your way through.

It was just here — between the herb garden and the start of the hydrangeas, white by the fence, pink nearer the patio — that Akii sited his first hive of bees last summer. He had attended several workshops and classes in Nagano and Tokyo, and worked with a beekeeper near Kyoto, and also his uncle, a Buddhist priest with a temple in Wakayama Prefecture who had several hives.

The bees — the Japanese variety known as *nihon mitsubachi* — came from Kawasaki, arriving while I was in the UK. I'm not saying they flew in unannounced, but rather they travelled in style by car in a cardboard carton.

Smaller than European bees, and far more amenable, they spent the summer very happily, gathering and accumulating so much nectar that Akii had to add a second box.

But then something went wrong.

Mites began to infect the combs and spoil the honey, and despite Akii scrubbing and doing his best to understand what was happening, the colony began to weaken.

By September, only the Queen and five worker bees were left.

The following week, the hive was empty.

It was the same week that Akii's father died, so a tough time.

Though whether my husband was more upset by the demise of his dad (which brought amid the sadness and sense of loss a certain amount of relief to all concerned, especially Akii who had nursed him to the end) or the inexplicable cot deaths of all his 'babies', would be hard to say.

Bees are dying all around the world; close neighbours in Scotland — Paul (dyker, tree planter and Congo insect expert) and his wife Ena — say their daughter who lives in Kenya lost many of her hives in much the same way.

Just beyond the hydrangeas, right now, in June, coming into flower stands a white metal table and four chairs, two of which match the table's pseudo-Victorian style, and the others in lightweight aluminium, picked up for next to nothing from Kura Kura; all they needed were new rubber stoppers on their feet from the local hardware store in Zushi and they were back in business.

They rest in the curve of the garden from where it is now a straight run to the driveway.

We sit out here often, for tea or coffee or a summer drink in the evening, mosquitoes allowing. Despite cleaning out the *hibachi* filled with water lilies and pondweed, to kill off eggs laid, they are always nearly intolerable once rainy season arrives.

Mind you, it arrived early this year, in late May, and no invasion yet.

There are pots of geraniums, red and white and pink. Between two trees a bamboo pole is hung with baskets of flowers and ferns. A white magnolia, flowers long gone and now in full leaf, offers relief from the sun.

Sounds pretty?

It is. Very.

Except of course for all the overhead cables and wires that litter the skyline in every direction. While buried underground in many more geologically stable countries, here everything is above ground, so theoretically making repairs after earthquakes, typhoons and landslides quicker and cheaper to facilitate.

Together the house and garden cover some fifty *tsubo*. This is the standard measure in Japan, one tsubo being about the same size as two tatami mats, that is, 3.3 metres square. Even though tatami are no longer considered mandatory in the construction of new homes, or remakes of old, the measure continues.

It's funny, but people — and this includes many Japanese — say I know a lot about Japan. The truth is I know only what I know, the tiniest tip imaginable of an iconic iceberg of immense size, age, depth and mystery. Every time I learn something new, I am reminded of how little I know.

But let me relax into the familiarity of this immediate comfort zone, sit with my back to the shrubs, and face the stretch along the front of the house, which is shaded with a veranda past the guest room to where the dining room ends and the *engawa* begins. It stands on rusting metal posts, with a roof of degraded corrugated plastic, but is nicer than it sounds; as is the crazy paved flooring.

Two folding chairs lean against the wall, rusted to a hue that blends nicely with the rustic nature of the garden at large; a bamboo wind chime hangs from a hook and, if not taken down, drives us mad through typhoons and strong winds off the sea.

Sonia brought it back from one of her F1 racing trips to Southeast Asia, but so long ago that it often falls to pieces. Undaunted, I simply re-string the thing and back up it goes.

Amusing also to spy two dumb-bells half-hidden under a clump of the variegated grass — a form of bamboo — that is coming up just about everywhere this year. I am supposed to fill them with water for working out, but never do.

Out of sight, out of mind.

What else is here? Lilies, irises, roses, a maple in one ceramic planter, lavender in another, low pots of pansies . . . And yet another hibachi, this time collecting water from the roof to keep pot plants alive through summery extremes of heat, heat, and more heat. (August I have to say, is near intolerable.)

I stand up and start along the path of stepping stones, with the veranda on the left, a wide border of trees and grass and shrubs to the right, and the nasty wire fence that separates us from Nonaka-san's property.

The bench came from Hayama; Shoi brought it on top of his car. When the garden in front of our house there was clear-cut and everything demolished, I rescued it. When Roberto mended one of its legs, he declared it one of the best designs he had ever seen, and made sketches so that he could knock out replicas.

Now, painted anew by Jeff, it is often used . . . by smokers who remove themselves from the house to feed this particular addiction, children and party-people who like to hang out, and readers and quiet-seeking souls like myself.

But what is this, on top of the white air conditioner unit that hums its way through summer, but only on the most unbearable of days? Being the same colour, the carving (from some kind of stone)

always comes as a surprise, found so long ago that I have quite forgotten where, when or how. A *semi*, or cicada, sits on three bean pods, maybe wisteria but hard to be sure.

Semi: one of THE sounds of summer. These extraordinary insects spend seven years underground before pushing upwards into the light as what are called 'nymphs', mating, laying eggs and then climbing trees to cast off their exoskeletons. The sound of these brittle cast-off skins crunching underfoot is discomforting, but children collect them with enthusiasm.

Mone, Rika's daughter, once decorated her sunhat with a row stitched along the brim. Japanese children are raised to appreciate insects, not be afraid of them. Just as the colour black is regarded as full of potential, and therefore positive; in the West, negative, negative, negative.

Other sounds mark different seasons, and once again encourage me list just a few of the things I would miss from my life here:

The fireworks off Zushi beach in summer . . .

Sitting on the sand with an ice-cold Corona beer in hand, watching the sun set behind Fuji-san across Sagami Bay . . .

Hearing the first bush warbler (*uguisu*) of spring echoing up and down the valley . . .

The chanting of monks as they go door to door collecting alms . . .

Falling asleep on tatami in hot sweaty weather to the sound of rain falling during *tsuyu* . . .

The ecstatic screaming of *mukudori*, a variety of starling, that gorge on ripe persimmon (*kaki*) in autumn . . .

The scattering of camellia petals that decorate the sloping approach to our home during winter. (There is always colour, even in snowfall: oranges and lemons through the year-end, with plum blossom and sweet-scented *suisen* from January on . . .

Drinking warming *amazake* (a drink made from the lees of rice in sake production) around a fire at our local shrine, Kuma-nojinja, named after the bears that used to roam the hillsides, and exchanging greetings with neighbours at *o-shogatsu* (new year) . . .

I could go on and on and on... wondering once again what happened to the CD *Water Dripping in a Dish: sounds of the Japanese city of Kyoto*, compiled by a German resident, that I ordered many years before, but which has since gone walkabout. Now Jalte has moved on and I have only the cover, which while a great sadness is better than nothing:

Kyoto is a noisy city, he writes. *At first I defended myself against the permanent din in the streets, the constant background music in department stores and the penetrating loudspeaker voices in trains.*

Then I started to collect noises and sounds. It turned into a voyage of discovery.

And I began to pay attention to the silence between the sounds.

Because, between those larger intrusive sounds are smaller ones, like water dripping in a dish . . .

Just as between larger unlovely objects are smaller more delightful ones, like a small flower, or a shard of blue and white china . . .

The ground is mostly mossy here, which I have been cheering on over the years, further encouraged by an Okinawan terracotta fish dangling on a chain from a branch, the small carved relief of a Hindu goddess propped against a trunk with a glass for occasional cut flowers, and a small stone lantern.

Just where the veranda ends are shrubs and a clump of day lilies, and a stone water-bath for birds. Then more grass, and eventually, between the tatami room and Akii's study, another hibachi in a bed of roses, azaleas, bulbs and a splendid maple, with dark crenellated leaves. There is also a lone traditional roof tile, standing to attention for no other reason than it looks good there.

This area of the garden always looks especially lovely in spring, with the white flowering shrub — which in full bloom resembles a mound of snow *(Spiraea Japonica)* — that Akii is especially fond of. He likes small white flowers, and anything in yellow.

On the other side, the border ends in first a monumental stone lantern, and then a giant Imperial-yellow and green-glazed Chinese planter with dragons writing around the sides, rescued from a garden down below when the owner tore down the lovely Taisho Period house to create a larger plot.

Sonia and I think the plan may have been to build a new house for a family member, but nothing has happened yet, allowing the garden to mature over the years into loveliness.

At the time, though, when the demolition team moved in and once again everything was being smashed up and dumped, it was AJ to the rescue: I rolled it up the hill one evening under cover of darkness.

It made me a kind of thief, I suppose, but with good intentions. Honest, guv.

Now it's planted with ivy, and stands below the tree that in Japanese style has been shaped so that one branch extends out over the driveway as if offering both protection and a welcome.

This is where the gardener that Asano-san sends in spring to prune and keep the trees in particular under strict control, always starts his work. He climbs up wearing rubber-soled *tabi* (split-toed shoes), Japanese shears in hand, and sets to work, clip, snip, snipping.

Poor Kobayashi-san.

I do give him a hard time, but that is because he approaches gardening differently to me.

All cultural, of course.

His is tough love. My own, sentimental.

And it all came to a head after I planted a climbing shrub with

orange trumpet flowers that I especially like, at the base of an old camellia. Sited in the bed across the other side of the drive, along with white, red and pink azaleas, this particular camellia had never borne flowers, so I thought the pairing quite clever.

Kobayashi-san, however, took one look and cut it through at the base.

While initially furious, stamping about like a frustrated child, I finally had to acknowledge that he was only thinking how best to bring the camellia back to health. And further drainage of its energies was perhaps not in its best interests.

In fact, we both got our way, because not only did I encourage the creeper to re-shoot and then hid the stem with rice matting (to protect it through the winter . . . my explanation and I'm sticking to it) but the host is in better shape than before. So we are both expecting great things this summer.

There is one more bed of shrubs, around the corner of the house which contains Akii's room, with a wooden sitting area in front. Called *nure-en*, it runs the full-length of the window into his study, allowing him to slide back the glass from inside and sit outside. With *nure* meaning 'getting wet', and *en* a Buddhist word describing the relationship between things, this seating could be thought of as an exterior engawa, open to all weathers.

There is another maple, this time with paler pinkish-brown and far more feathery leaves; also a tall evergreen with drifts of long hanging pine needles. These too are bonsai-ed every year, always to stunning effect.

There is, however, one shrub that I prefer to look after myself, and Kobayashi-san seems to have learned to respect that need in me, if no other.

When I was a child growing up in Coventry, my mother planted a coral pink Japonica along the front wall of our 1930s semi-detached house. She had never been to Japan, but it was always her dream to visit, which by great fortune (and exceptional fortitude) she was able to make a reality while still fit enough to get around.

Imagine my delight then to find a similar shrub here, in much the same position, when we arrived.

It was spectacular this spring.

She is very happy, I believe, to see it thriving in this fashion, in this place, along with her daughter.

Be grateful for the home you have,
knowing that at this moment,
all you have is all you need.
Sarah Ban Breathnach

LEAVE-TAKING

sayohnara, dewa mata, mata ne

It is always hard to say goodbye, but in this instance there is no need. We can come back any time ... through these words, if not physically.

The gate is open, for Alex, who is leaving his bicycle here now that the old bike parking space just behind the station has been turned into a pricey electronic playground for the affluent gadget-minded.

Amazing to see how the spaces cleared for building have been taken over by green again; no-one is going to buy the plots, not at the prices being asked. And if the owner intends to wait for the economy to improve, I fear he or she may be in for the long haul. That leaves us pretty happy, in this respect at least.

As to Samurai-san's house, down to the right, past Nonaka san's gate, it has been made over. Samurai-san moved on, and with the place empty, the elderly owner, who is also Sonia and Yuta's landlord, decided to transform it into his summer *bessoh* (holiday house).

It was all being done very tastefully too . . . until two crystal chandeliers were hung in the modest living room.

Now the front garden is disappearing under a neat arrangement of bricks and tiles and holes for parasols, so Kato-san can sit outside and read.

Has anyone told him about the mosquitoes? we wonder.

Sonia is sad to have lost the lovely *matsu* (pine tree) that overhung the path to her front door; as she says, only the Japanese would chainsaw down such a cultural icon without a second thought.

And now the splendid figure of Samurai-san striding down towards the road, pony tail topknot twirling, divided skirt-like trousers (*hakama*) swinging, has been replaced by a sadder figure, who often sits on a bench in front of Sekisui Heights, the two-

storey block of small apartments down the slope on the corner to the road, waiting . . .

Waiting for his elderly partner to come home from shopping, a charming elderly woman who had just begun visiting us, but died suddenly last year.

Many changes. Some expected. Others not.

The Ogasawara Islands are now a fully protected World Heritage site.

Catherine is now on Salt Spring Island, Vancouver, working as a gardener.

Brendan and his son are in Ireland A very happy ending, or beginning . . . He has also finished his book.

I did empty the bottle of *umeshu* on the compost heap, leaving the garden smelling like a brewery for weeks.

I do have a new pencil sharpener.

I did find a home for the African collage in the downstairs *nando*.

Yoko, a dentist and one of my Tuesday evening English

students in Numama, Higashi-Zushi, surprised us all in class a week or so ago by announcing she had got married. When she brought her new husband for tea Sunday last, I offered it, knowing she had an interest in all things African; she rode off with the collage on the back of his motorbike, clutching it in triumph.

Other things have been given away, or sorted for charity and recycle shops.

Writing this has been very good in this respect alone: I have seen how much stuff I have accumulated and acknowledged how much is redundant . . . even things I thought I would/could never part from are seen now in a different light.

I have always loved creating homes . . . and I have never been comfortable in ugly spaces surrounded by what I consider to be ugly things.

Beauty is of course always in the eye of the beholder, and in this

respect I guess I am a bit like Meryl Streep's baroness in the film *Out of Africa* (based on the book by the Danish writer Karen Blixen, aka Isak Dinesen) who, when teased for her strong attachment to her Limoges china and fine linen (and that cuckoo clock!) transported all the way from Denmark to Kenya, says simply, without apology: "I like my things".

We all like our things, and the sense of security — however delusional — that they bring. I remember watching my mother sort and throw, sort and throw in her declining years, readying for what she called Popping Off.

She knew something that we did not; on some inexplicable level she knew who she was, and what or who she was going to become, without stuff.

When belongings are taken away forcibly, though, it is often a shock from which many never recover, as if it were those things that gave them their identity. I often ask writers to reflect on who they are without their back story. It is this strength of self-knowledge that allows people to start again if needs be.

I have started several times in my life from scratch and always with an initial sense of panic. But taken minute-by-minute, day-by-day, it always comes right.

The last time was after my South American trip.

Before that? When I sold up to come to Japan.

Now I guess I can do so again if needs be.

My sense is that in writing about this house and the life created inside it, I have to some extent written my way out of it, past it, through it. A good thing, I believe, because things are only things, and as the old saying goes, you can't take it with you when you go.

I will take my leave with pleasure and gratitude for the visit, and by repeating the paragraph I wrote at the end of the introduction, six months ago, because it proved prophetic. By now you are sure to have caught on as to why, but just in case not, what I was offering was:

A simple love story, no more, no less . . .

Because we may not be here much longer, and even if we stay in Japan, life is shifting, the world in transition, and I want to remember.

Remember it all.

ACCEPTING CHANGE, BOWING OUT, EMBRACING TRANSITION (2012)

As you know, I began this book in late September 2010, ostensibly to set the pace for students in their writing projects. By the end of the eight-week course I was halfway through. Then came Christmas, New Year, a trip to Toronto, and another quickie to Scotland to help my aunt move permanently into a residential home in Perth. During this period, I was writing bits and pieces, creeping forward paragraph by paragraph, but with momentum dissipated the focus had fallen away, was just not there.

Three days after arriving back from London, the northeast coast of Honshu, Japan's largest island in the archipelago, was impacted by one of the most powerful earthquakes on record. This was swiftly followed by a tsunami that swept away whole communities, with near 20,000 deaths accounted for and many still missing. As if these two tragedies were not enough, we now know that at least three of the reactors at the Daiichi Nuclear Plant in Fukushima went into meltdown, creating a situation now acknowledged as being far worse than that facing Chernobyl in the spring of 1986. Just this morning, we heard that radiation levels after the plant was initially overwhelmed by seawater, were well over twice those initially reported.

Akii and I were in Kyoto when the Chernobyl disaster was first reported. It was raining, and I remember that over breakfast, we were instructed by radio and TV to take our umbrellas if going outside, to help protect us from radiation.

Akii was on his bike, between Numama and Zushi, when the quake struck Japan on Friday, March 11 at 3:25 pm. He subsequently spent twelve hours with no electricity or means of communication (even mobile phones were not working), and more than a few more not knowing if I was dead or alive. Eventually he was able to learn that I had left NHK in Shibuya where I was working in the AsiaVision satellite ops room and presumably was trying to find a way home, like the millions of others in the capital faced with the closure of the entire rail network. In fact I was fine — or as fine as anyone could be in such circumstances — eventually returning home twenty-four hours later.

By this time the reactors had begun to explode.

On Sunday evening Lee rang late from London imploring me to leave the area, fast. Fearing he knew something we did not (true, as it turned out), we left early the next morning: with rail links into Tokyo closed down, we had to make a long circulatory journey to eventually find a way to take the *shinkansen* bullet train south. After three days in Wakayama Prefecture, with Akii's cousin's son and family finally having accumulated enough petrol to start fleeing Fukushima as radiation refugees, we felt homesick and foolish and came back.

Thousands had survived but seen their homes snatched away by a relentless wall of water, which then dragged everything dear back into the depths of the ocean. Many thousands more were being evacuated from an ever-widening zone for fear of radiation leaks; no choice here — and harder in a way because they were having to abandon their ways of life and leave their homes, businesses, pets and livestock, all because of an invisible enemy.

With our home intact, we had no reason not to return, so we did. Which of course many abroad could not understand, believing, in the light of what we thought at the time were scare-mongering reports by the foreign media, that such a move had to be even more idiotic. But I wanted to go back, to be among my books and music and friends and, in large part, because I felt a strong sense of urgency — the strong need — to finish this.

And so we have hung on, living a relatively normal life in

abnormal circumstances, doing the best we can. I do have a very strong memory, however, of leaving the house for Kansai that Monday morning with one rucksack and a handbag to my name — about the same amount of luggage with which I had arrived in Japan twenty-five years ago — and again choosing not to look back.

Akii kept stopping to turn around but I could not. It was too painful . . . I really did consider it a distinct possibility that we might never return. At that time though I was clear and resolute: it was a pity I had not completed the book, but too late, everything could go.

Now a few of the stories that have framed my life in Japan to date are mapped out. There is so much that I learned on my household walkabout, and for all such remembrances and revelations I am truly grateful.

I am grateful also to the insurance company who (through the auspices of our landlady) paid up for damage caused by a typhoon in late autumn. The roof tiles have been re-laid after many crashed to the ground, causing a large-scale re-shifting; the old corrugated plastic roof over the terrace has been replaced; the shutter to the cave and the bridge are gone, removed. Less romantic, but a whole lot safer.

If it were not for the tremors that continue to rattle our bones and our nerves, that is. One of the latest larger aftershocks was in the foothills of Mt Fuji, which is definitely too close for comfort. The whole of Japan is under ongoing stress, on just about every level imaginable.

Yes, anxiety is a constant companion these days, but on occasion making me appreciate as never before what it is I have, am privy to.

After reading an interview with a nuclear expert that made my hair stand on end, for example . . . Most of the time we have been complaining about the lack of hard information; suddenly here was more than I challenge anyone to handle with equanimity.

Having turned seventy earlier in the week, at the end of May, I had saved champagne and cheese until the weekend.

As I took that first sip, the atmosphere in the room changed, swelled. There was an intensity, an immediacy . . . I remember thinking, maybe I will never taste this again, and rolling the liquid around my mouth and over my tongue as if savouring it as never before.

A crumb of cheese nearly blew my taste buds away; what if suddenly there were no cheese-makers — just as now in Fukushima and adjoining prefectures, whole industries have gone to the wall — even if producers do make tofu, sake, *kamaboko* (boiled fish paste), will anyone eat it, for fear of contamination?

Never have slices of imported Stilton, Emmental and Camembert tasted so voluptuous.

The sensation of the hand-forged knife in my hand was cool and marvellously smooth; an extraordinarily beautiful object in itself.

The fabric of the chair on which I was sitting felt the most sensuous imaginable.

While, in profile, Akii became the prince I had not seen in him for years.

The air in the room was thick with love, colours subtly vibrating and yet vivid in distinction. As environmentalist and author Rachel Carson (*The Silent Spring*) once encouraged, I was wholly focussed on seeing, feeling, hearing, smelling and touching as if for "the first and last time".

This mini-awakening — Eckhart Tolle calls it a "peak experience" — lasted no more than fifteen minutes or so, but it brought home the import, value and beauty of trying to live fully in each and every moment.

Because, as writing this has proved, you never know . . .

Who would have thought in the autumn of 2010, when I set out to write a love story about 'things', that they would become so relatively unimportant?

Travelling back from London in July 2011, I shared a few words with an American and his children traveling from Miami to South Africa. On hearing I was returning to Japan, he assumed that, since there was nothing in the news these days (due to Japanese government pressure, it needs to be said), everything had to be okay now, returned to normal.

Explaining that Japan had a new normal that was far from being clear and understood, he became very still and then added quietly, "Is it my imagination, or is everything speeding up while at the same time everything we take for granted is breaking down?"

His comment was very observant, very timely, for that coming year promised to pack more and more prescient punches, and none from directions we were expecting. We were warned, but the large majority prefer to ignore messages left by the ancients, just as Japanese ignored the many inscribed tsunami stones erected all along the coast over the centuries: Learn through our experience, they read; do not build below this point.

On the cusp of 2012, it feels important to work out what to leave behind — for my part, fear (not easy, I can assure you) — and what best to carry forward into future unknown —what the Canadian Buddhist nun Pema Chodron calls "gentle courage".

I leave therefore with that wise saying of old that continues to survive the test of time: *The past is history, the future is a mystery, now is a gift, and that's why it's called the present.*

My heart broke this (last year). But I am not broken. Wherever I am, I am home. No matter where.

Which is why I can say, Let it go, Angela. Let it all go . . .

ZUSHI, 28 DECEMBER 2011

Where thou art, that is home.
Emily Dickinson

EPILOGUE

We left Japan for Perthshire, in Scotland, for a number of inter-related reasons. I went first, in the October of 2012, and so was able to spend the last two months of her life with my last surviving older relative. As for Akii, after many trials and tribulations, he was finally granted a spouse visa that enabled him to celebrate the closing days of the year in Scotland. Technically "retired", it made sense to give up renting in Japan and move to a place we are fortunate enough to be able to call our own.

Now based in the cottage (a converted croft) that my mother lived in for over forty years until her death, down-along the road from her younger sister, the idea was to come here for twelve months and see how things progressed . . .

Many of the items described in the previous pages have moved with us. But others have settled into new homes, back in Japan.

Mary took the mannequin from the porch.

Ruthie carried away the US-made ironing board; she'd been improvising for years.

Most of the quilts went to evacuation centres in Tohoku; quilt tops were gifted to former Japanese students at a wonderful and very emotional sayonara party in Zushi.

Alex now has the matching chair from the *engawa*.

The garden bench is back along the coast, with Shoi and Colleen in Akiya.

The rattan chair, bought for my mother's visit, today hangs out with Kathryn in her beloved Tokyo.

Jacinta took a smaller version – a small woven bucket chair - on the local train to her weekend pad in Misaki; I have a photo of her sitting on it, while all the Japanese passengers pretend not to notice.

Rainer was happy to take Brenda home. While he now reports regularly of cycling happily up and down and around Kamakura, just as I did once-upon-a-wonderful-time, I am equally happy knowing she is in such good hands.

Rika thought to take the cheap metal Thai teapot, but at the last minute decided against; it would upset her too much.

Kristin helped me sift through all published writings, and in particular, decide which *Japan Times* articles to keep and which to let go . . .

Innumerable smaller things are now in use by the Ito family . . .

Yes, we know where everyone and everything is, should we decide to return (just joking . . .)

For the time being at least, though, we remain here.

ACKNOWLEDGEMENTS

Thank you from the bottom of my heart to all participants here and there in Japan . . . and all those who have moved on from the timeline of these tales:

(*Informally, and roughly in alphabetical order*)
Alan White; Alena Ecklemann; Alex, Rikako & Nina Reid; Amanda & Marianne (as were); Andy & Joan Melia; Astrid de los Rios, Azzah Manukova; Barry & Debbie Bliss; Beatrix Schilcher; Betty Barnden; Bill Bailey; John Bowstead; Brenda Tierney; Brendan Conway; Bruno Groening-Circle of Friends; Buffy Jeffs & Ross Waddell & Max; Byron Monasmith; Caterina Dorello; Catharine Fried (1937-2015); Catharine & Koichi Nagashima; Catherine Reid; Chiaki Takahashi; Chris & Shirley Macdonald; Christine Farris; Clara Birnbaum; David Reynolds; Deirdre Seresin; Demi & John Daub; Diana & Jim Buyer; Dr Betty Edwards; Duncan McLean & Ingrid Tait & Cara; Emi Tanabe; Ena Richards; Florence Kiribi; Freddie Robbins; Gaku Naito (& Mariko Kainuma); Geoffrey Tudor; George Bussey; Glen Taylor; Goli Pastobar; Graham (& Bo) Harper); Hani Mazour; Heather Willson; Hiroko Iwashita & Craig Akers; Humphrey Evans & Ros Spry; Ingrid Mason; Isabel Moore; Jacinta Hin; James Heartland & Reiko Kanno Heartland; James Howard; Jane Garten; Janis Stewart; Jacqui McLennan (& Tony Rickaby); Jeff Mulberry; Jeffrey Jouson; Jill Fanshawe-Kato (& Setsuo Katoh); Jill Hood; Jillian Yorke; Joseph Schwarz; Joy Suzuki; John Beirne; John Harding; Josephine D. Speid (1910-2012); Judi Goodwin; Kara Wilson; Karen Gertsbrein; Kathryn Matsumura; Kazuko Tanaka & family; Kei Yokoyama; Ken Joseph Jr (Japan Help Line); Kiki

Bragard; Kristin Newton; Lee Jeffs & Susan Crown; Leah Seresin; Leesa & Don Gawlik Zanelli; Leonardo, Shinobu, Mina & Marino Benucci; Lia Howe; Liga Pang; Linda Cole; Louise Egerton & Fred Magro; Maki Uchida; Malte Jaspersen; Mamoru Hatta; Mark Silver; Mary Fidler; Masako Asano & family; Meira Chand; Merry Angel; Michael Ho; Michelle Young & Richard Crane (Passe-Partout); Michiyo Masago; Naoko Matsubara; Nikolas Dixon (& Adam Radomsky); Omar Garcia; Paul Norris; Patsy North; Paul & Ena Latham; Paul John Murray; Peter Popham; Petra Fried; Rassanikon Nanong; Rainer Zandrock; Ray Barlin; Rika Wakame (& Mone); Rita Tempel; Roberto Takeyama; Roger Jeffs; Rosie Tucker; Ruben Saufkie; Ruthie Iida; Sachiko Yatani; Sandra Matsumoto; Sandy Black; Sandy Carr Cleland & John Cleland; Sarah & Adrian Murray-Bradley; Shiho Ichinoi-Suzuki; Shoi & Colleen Sakurai; Sonia, Yuta & Julia Ito; Sumiko Honma; Susannah Thomkins; Taizaburo Yamamura; Takehiro Naito; Tateo & Hiroki (as were); Tomoko Tanaka/TGA Inc; Vincent (Vin) Morris; Vivian & David Lowe; Wakiko Noguchi; Yasue Horie; Yoko Maebara; Yoshiko Shimabukuro; Yuko Makishi; Yumi Uemura

Even larger lavishly colourful and aromatic bouquets of thanks to Jacinta Hin, Kathryn Matsumura and Kristin Newton for feedback; Robert Kidd for initial editing; Jillian Yorke for ongoing editorial support and all the additional nitpicking; and once again, Alan White for layout and design.

Also, for their exceedingly apt quotations, gratitude and respect to author James Salter (from his book *Burning the Days*), graphic and textile designer Erin Flett, writer and philosopher Sarah Ban Breathnoch, the Literary Estate of poet Emily Dickinson, and Japanese literary phenomenon Haruki Murakami (from his third novel, *A Wild Sheep Chase*).

GLOSSARY

ai : indigo dyestuff

aizome : ikat dyeing technique using indigo

ame : sweets

amado : outside wooden window shutters that slide to and fro

amazake : hot alcoholic beverage made from rice lees

andon : lamp

asa : hemp

bashou-fu : textile woven from banana plantain fibres

bashou : banana plantain

bessou : weekend or holiday house

bonsai : the controlled miniaturisation of trees grown in containers

-hori, -bori : wood carving

-chan : affectionate honorific for young girls and anything
  someone is fond of

daidokoro : kitchen

deshi : apprentice, disciple

dewa mata : until we meet again

dozo yoroshiku : how do you do, please (enter/come in)

daininguruumu : dining room (as pronounced and written
  in the phonetic alphabet katakana)

danchi : state housing, usually high-rise

engawa : the room space between the inside and the outside

fuu sui : feng shui: auspicious interior and exterior principles
  of design (Chinese in origin)

fuji : wisteria (the ideographic kanji character for Mt Fuji,
  or Fuji-san, is different)

furoshiki : carrying or wrapping cloth

fusuma : papered sliding doors, used to partition or close
    off rooms

futatsu : two (futatsume: second, number two)

gaikokujin : literally 'outsider'; 'gaijin' as slang for foreigner

genkan : entrance hall

genmai : whole (brown) rice

gokiburi : cockroach

gomi : rubbish

haiku : 17-syllable three-line poem

hakama : divided skirt traditionally worn by men

hanga : wood block print

hanko : seal used instead of signature

hanten : quilted jacket worn in winter

hashira : square-cut supportive pillar

heya : room

hibachi : ceramic or metal container for charcoal (the traditional
    form of heating)

hiragana : phonetic alphabet used to link *kanji*

hitotsu : one (*hitotsume*: first, number one)

hora-ana : cave

igusa : reed used to cover tatami matting

ikebana : traditional flower arranging

irasshaimase : welcome

iro-iro : this and that

izakaya : pub

jinguu : shrine

kaidan : staircase

kaki : persimmon fruit

kamaboko : steamed fish paste

kamidana : it. 'god shelf'

kamon (mon) : clan or family crest

kanji : ideographs imported from China in the fifth century

kannon : goddess of mercy

kasuri : traditional textile, with natural fibres pre-dyed in indigo
(*ai*) to allow pattern to form in the weaving

katana : sword

katakana : syllabic alphabet used for spelling out all non-Japanese
words

kawaii : cute, attractive and appealing

kawara : roof tile

keigo : polite, honorific Japanese

kenjutsu : swordsmanship

kirei : clean, fresh, attractive

kouban : neighbourhood police box

kome : de-husked white rice

kotatsu : low table with heating unit and removable quilt, used
in winter

kun : affectionate male honorific

kuzu : kudzu vine

maiko : apprentice/student geisha in Kyoto

manga : comic book

maru : circle

mata ne : *S*ee you! (very colloquial)

matsu : pine tree

matsuri : festival

meishi : business/name card

mikoshi : portable Shinto shrine, in which gods are believed
to reside

mingei : folk crafts movement in Japan, officially established
in 1926; in large part inspired by the Arts and Crafts
Movement in Britain and Europe

minshuku : bed and breakfast, Japanese style

miso : fermented soy beans

mittsu : three (mittsume: third, number three)

mon : gate/gateway

mukudori : bird from starling family

nando : store room

naruhodo : I see/understand

netsuke : tiny sculptures carved from ivory, boxwood, etc., and hung from the sashes of men's kimono; much prized

nengajou : cards sent at New Year

nihongo : Japanese language

nihonjin : Japanese person

nihon mitsubachi : Japanese honey bees

niwa : garden

noren : divided curtains hung outside shops and restaurants to signify they are open for business

nure-en : outside seat

obaachan : affectionate name for an elderly woman

obi : sash worn with kimono

ocha : green tea

ofuro : bathroom

omiyage : semi-obligatory gift or souvenir

omote : woven covering of *tatami*

onsen : hot spring

oshiire : cupboard behind sliding door or doors (*fusuma*)

ranma : decorative divider above doorways between rooms, often pierced to allow air to circulate

rakugo : traditional storytelling; literally 'falling words' and referring to the 'fall' (as opposed to a punchline) at the end of the story

rouka : corridor

saka/zaka : slope

samue : traditional monk's clothing or work clothing

san : honorific for men and women, like Mr or Mrs

sashiko : running stitch

satori : enlightenment, as sought in Zen Buddhism

sayounara : goodbye

sensei : eacher, or master (professor, medical doctor)

seitai : body adjustment

semi : cicada

sen-en : thousand-yen note

senko : incense

sentou : public bath

shinkansen : high speed 'Bullet' train

shintou : Japan's animist (nature-based) religion

shouchuu : rice liquor; cheaper than sake

shougun : literally, head of military

shosai : study/workroom

shouji : papered door or screen to allow for privacy and soft light

soba : buckwheat noodles

sobagara : buckwheat husks

sodai gomi : big rubbish

suisen : fragrant winter narcissus

sumi : black ink

sushi-oke : wooden cask for making sushi rice

susuki : pampas-like grass

tabi : footwear with split toes

take : bamboo

tako-yaki : popular snack of bits of octopus cooked in batter

takkyuubin : four-hour door-to-door delivery service

tanchoo-zuru : red-headed crane, a popular symbol of longevity and happiness

tansu : storage chest

tatami : traditional mat used as flooring

tenjou : ceiling

tenugui : narrow cotton towels or scarves, twisted and tied
    around the head as a sweat band, or as an act of
    empowerment

toire : toilet

tokonoma : art alcove

tombi : kite (feathered variety)

tsuyu : rainy season, traditionally from June to July

uchi : house

uguisu : bush warbler

umeshu : plum wine

umi no ie : temporary buildings on the beach in summer

urushi : lacquer

wabi sabi : a Japanese aesthetic linked to Zen Buddhism and the
    tea ceremony: wisdom and humility in simplicity

washi : handmade paper, originally made from mulberry leaves

washiki : Japanese-style

washitsu : Japanese-style room

yane : roof

yen : Japanese currency

youshitsu : Western-style

yottsu : four (yotsume: fourth, number four)

yukashita-shuunou : storage space below floor level

yukata : cotton bathrobe in kimono-style

zabuton : flat floor cushion

*Summer light, the smell of the breeze,
the sound of cicadas – if I like these things,
why should I apologise?*
Haruki Murakami

RECOMMENDED READING

To deepen your interest in and understanding of Japanese architecture and lifestyle:

Japanese Country Style, by Yoshihiro Takishita, published by Kodansha USA, 2002. *Lots of detail about traditional minka. (Recommended by Alex Kerr & Jonquil Melrose-Woodman)*

The Unknown Craftsman: A Japanese Insight into Beauty, by Soetsu Yanagi & Bernard Leach, published by Kodansha, 2013. *Mingei folk movement founder Yanagi (1889-1961) was the first to fully explore the traditional Japanese appreciation for "objects born, not made". (Recommended by Amy Sylvester Katoh)*

The Wabi-Sabi House: the Japanese Art of Imperfection, by Robin Griggs Laurence & Jo Cocca, published by Clarkson Potter, 2004. *More a mindset than about style. (Recommended by Jonquil Melrose-Woodman)*

Blue and White Japan, by Amy Sylvester Katoh & Yutaka Satoh, published by Tuttle, 1996. *The colours — sea, sky, dye — of Asia in glorious celebration . . . (Recommended by Catherine Reid)*

Living in Japan (Taschen), by Alex Kerr and Kathy Arlyn Sokol. *Coffee table book with photos of houses, traditional and modern. Very simple text. (Recommended by Koichi & Catharine Nagashima)*

Tokyo Style, with text and photographs by Kyoichi Tsuzuki, published by Kyoto Shoin, 1993. *A very personal "take"* on how Japanese live in a contemporary urban environment. *(Recommended by Angela Jeffs)*

To deepen your interest in and understanding of traditional Japanese gardens:

Japanese Garden Design, by Marc Peter Keane & Haruzo Ohashi, published by Tuttle, 2007. *The theory, history, and intricacies of Japanese gardening. (Recommended by Jonquil Melrose-Woodman & Mark Silver.)*

Sakuteiki: Visions of Japanese Gardening (A Tuttle classic of Japanese literature), published 2008. *Written over 1,000 years ago, this is the oldest known book on Japanese gardening. (Recommended by Noami Escudero-Oliver)*

Niwaki: Pruning, Training and Shaping Trees*, by Jake Hobbs,* **published by Timber Press, 2007.** *Based on traditional skills learned in a Japanese nursery, everything you need to know about the garden-equivalent of bonsai. (Recommended by Catherine Reid)*

General reading:

DK Eyewitness Travel Guide Japan, published by Dorling Kindersley, last updated edition 2015. *Good basic information presented in DK's trademark visual style. (Recommended by Angela Jeffs)*

The Forgotten Japanese: Encounters with Rural Life and Folklore, by Tsuneichi Miyamoto & Jeffrey Irish, published by Stone Bridge Press, 2010. *Japanese folklore scholar and rural advocate Miyamoto (1907-1981) walked 160,000 kilometres to* *conduct interviews and capture a dying way of life. (Recommended by Amy Sylvester Katoh & Brendan Conway)*

Wabi-sabi: For Artists, Designers, Poets and Philosophers, by Leonard Koren, published by Imperfect Publishing, 2008. *How true beauty can be seen in imperfection and incompletion, even decay. (Recommended by Jonquil Melrose-Woodman)*

Lost Japan, by Alex Kerr, re-published by Penguin, 2015. *For an understanding of changes since 1945, and traditional culture's trade-off for so-called development. A loving and informed account of a fast-disappearing world. (Recommended by James Howard)*

Strong In The Rain (Surviving Japan's Earthquake, Tsunami, and Fukushima Nuclear Disaster), by Lucy Birmingham & David McNeill. published by Palgrave Macmillan, 2012. *Journalistic writing at its best. (Recommended by Kristin Newton & Ruthie Iida)*

Fresh Currents, from the quarterly magazine Kyoto Journal – Perspectives from Asia. *A multi-authored inquiry into the consequences of Japan's mid-1950s decision to go nuclear: http://www.kyotojournal.org/backissues/fresh-currents/ (Recommended by Ruthie Iida & Jeffrey Jouson)*

Up from the Sea, by Leza Lowitz, published by Penguin Random House, 2016. *A young adult novel in verse about making a home within yourself when the only home you've ever known is destroyed. (Recommended by Jacinta Hin)*

Have you also read **Chasing Shooting Stars**?

Published in 2013 after ten years in the writing, this is far more than a month-long travelogue. It is a roller-coaster ride of emotions, an intriguing family history, and a sometimes painful personal memoir. Based on a journey made in 1999 to South America, it links three continents, three countries, and one hundred and seven letters written by Angela's paternal grandfather in Buenos Aires to her father in England. It is a true labour of love to find a far-flung family from the distant and not-so-distant past.

"My grandfather described the events of his life in Argentina and Uruguay, after his wife in Liverpool cast him out, as 'a mad romp'. Believe me, the trip I made – with no Spanish and little to no idea as to what I was going to do when I got there – beats his own hands down! But what an amazing learning curve . . ."

Print to order
by CreateSpace
on Amazon.com